The BRAVO! Way

The BRAVO! Way
Building a Southern Restaurant Dynasty

Dawn Dugle

A traditional publisher with a non-traditional approach to publishing

Copyright © 2018 by Dawn Dugle
Cover Design Credit: Suzi Jochimsen Hood
Library of Congress Control Number: 2018950522
ISBN: 978-1-941644-26-3

All rights reserved. This book or any portion thereof may not be reproduced or used in any manner whatsoever without the express written permission of the publisher except for the use of brief quotations in a book review. WARNING: Unauthorized duplication or downloading is a violation of applicable laws. File sharing is allowed only with those companies with which Sartoris Literary Group has a written agreement.

Sartoris Literary Group, Inc.
Jackson, Mississippi
www.sartorisliterary.com

Dedicated to all of us who are running with scissors

CONTENTS

Foreword

CHAPTER 1: Jackson Calling
13

CHAPTER 2: Get to Yes
41

CHAPTER 3: Che è Per Pranzo
77

CHAPTER 4: The Middle Child
105

CHAPTER 5: Do the Right Thing
134

CHAPTER 6: Yin and Yang
154

CHAPTER 7: Speak Truth to Power
180

CHAPTER 8: The BRAVO! Way
202

Acknowledgements
228

Foreword

"For I have known them all already, known them all:
Have known the evenings, mornings, afternoons,
I have measured out my life with coffee spoons;
I know the voices dying with a dying fall
Beneath the music from a farther room."
"The Love Song of J. Alfred Prufrock" by T. S. Eliot

The restaurant business is a demanding mistress and a powerful foe. She can grind the strongest to dust with the daily repetition of events: open, prepare, serve, clean up, close. Like Eliot's character Prufrock, the significance of a restaurant is not measured by one stellar review, or any given record night of sales, rather it is built one transaction at a time – one meal, one coffee spoon at a time. The successful restaurateur must be able to handle one thousand details at once, each with care and precision, each laying a foundation on which the next day's service, and the next, and the next, will be built.

We first met Dawn Dugle as a guest. As a local television executive, she would often dine at BRAVO! with clients and quickly became known as the "lady who loves the chocolate torte". It became a pattern for Dawn to "call ahead" and make sure we had the Flourless Chocolate Torte prior to her visit, and she would claim the last piece if necessary. She was hooked.

As with many restaurant owner/customer relationships, familiarity led to friendship, friendship led to sharing, and sharing ultimately led to this; a book about our business, our friendship and our beliefs. Our story has been decades in the making, yet Dawn has masterfully distilled it to eight chapters, each with a different lens to the organism, much like an MRI takes layered slices of pictures to see the secrets of the whole.

We met in High School in 1980 when Jeff moved to Jackson as a result of a new job for his dad. Dan extended a helping hand after an awkward moment in the classroom for Jeff. From that moment forward, we have been inseparable even when distance, time or conflict has tried to separate us. We have built an award-winning trio of restaurants from scratch, raising the funds to do so in a most creative, and unorthodox way. We employ nearly 200 people and we serve close to a million meals each year. Still, our overarching philosophies of "every plate is a face" and "do the right thing" guide our actions, and those of our team members.

We are in the customer service business where guest care and satisfaction is gauged and measured continuously, and often publicly, through internet rating sites and widespread social media use. If we don't get it right, we hear about it. And so does the rest of the world.

The BRAVO! Way: Building a Southern Restaurant Dynasty is a 100 percent accurate telling of story; our ups, our downs, the personalities that have cycled through our doors, the idiosyncrasies of each of us as business partners and as unique individuals, the finances behind our businesses, the failures we have endured, and the triumphs we have celebrated. It is our story, told through the eyes of a most talented storyteller, someone trained in getting the who/what/where/when/why/how into a succinct package for the news.

Dawn has lived in six different states and a foreign country. She has fearlessly gone where the stories and the opportunities have led her. Whether writing for a newscast, managing an entire news team or working for a business development entity, Dawn has consistently left her mark of excellence and passion prior to moving on to the next tour of duty. An opportunity in broadcast journalism leadership led her to the city of Jackson, the capital of Mississippi. For this blonde, fair-skinned Hoosier, Mississippi may have initially seemed foreign, but because we are the land of storytellers, it fit her like a glove.

She has bloomed in the Magnolia state, creating a life centered on a consulting and speaking business, which helps individuals find their inner passions and then share those stories with the rest of the world. Dawn travels the country, speaking to organizations and teaching them how to tell their stories, but she always returns home to Mississippi. She continuously builds her network of friends and collaborators by being present and authentic when she is with someone, and it's this authenticity that led us to open up our lives to her.

The BRAVO! Way: Building a Southern Restaurant Dynasty is Dawn Dugle's first book, and we could not have been luckier to have someone of her caliber tell our tale.

Jeff Good and Dan Blumenthal
Owners of BRAVO!, Broad Street and Sal & Mookie's

Wine with dinner at BRAVO! Photo © Tom and Kasi Beck, all rights reserved

CHAPTER 1

JACKSON CALLING

It's seven o'clock on a Friday night, and a whirlwind has descended on BRAVO! Italian Restaurant and Bar. It seems everyone in the dining room sat down at once, and with a chill in the November air, everyone is ordering hot food.

At first glance, the hot line in the kitchen is in total chaos—men shouting at each other, orange and blue flames leaping two feet high over the sauté station sending waves of heat through the kitchen, and clattering plates and pans drown out the sous chef as he calls for an order to be finished.

"I need another crusted fish!" he shouts.

"You got a crusted fish in the window," the head cook shouts back.

"No, I need *another* crusted fish," the sous chef insists.

"What about that crusted fish for 46?"

"This one's for 34!"

The cook turns to the hot line and shouts: "I need a crusted fish on the fly."

"Crusted fish—heard!" the floating cook shouts back. He knows he needs to move the entrée ahead of whatever else he is cooking and get it done ASAP. Customers are waiting. At BRAVO! once the order ticket comes into the kitchen, the goal is to get the hot food out to the table within eighteen minutes.

Everyone hustles to get the order completed, and the expeditor rushes the crabmeat-crusted fish over to the head cook, where he starts plating it.

"34 hitting the window," he shouts to the sous chef.

"34 in the window," he shouts seconds later. "Crusted fish in the window, sell it!"

The sous chef takes the order, garnishes it, and sets it on the counter for the waiter to rush it to the table.

What seems like total chaos at first is actually a well-choreographed dance. The expeditor calling out the orders to the line cooks. The line cooks dropping butter, wine or olive oil into pans then adding ingredients from drawers underneath the stoves. The fragrant smell of butter and garlic wafts through the kitchen. Flames from the gas stove flash high as the sauté cook flips the contents of one pan.

The dishwasher appears, dodging cooks to pick up dirty plates and pans to take them back to the "dish hole" for cleaning. The other sous chef walks through the narrow kitchen en route to the walk-in cooler to get something for the cold line. In between calling out orders, the cooks are in a constant state of smack talk and laughter. It's intense, but they love every minute of it.

Then, just as fast as it started, the whirlwind dies down. Flour, spices, butter, pasta and stove knobs litter the floor and counters. Dirty pans are stacked up and ready for another trip to the dish hole.

The BRAVO! kitchen is open to the restaurant, so the expeditor can see when people are about to leave, and when new customers will be seated.

He turns and gives a smile before shouting out: "We got another turn coming, reset!"

Everyone restocks their stations and wipes down countertops, ready for the next whirlwind.

In the lounge area, a crowd of customers waits to be seated for dinner. There is a young couple, in their teens, dressed for a big event. He doesn't look old enough to drive, but is wearing a tuxedo with a pink boutonniere. She's in a pink strapless gown, and shivers on this cold evening, having left her coat in the car. Both of them are wearing the awkwardness of a first date.

At the bar is an older couple wearing jeans and sweaters, silently sitting side-by-side. She's watching the people in the lounge, and absentmindedly traces the rim of her wine glass over and over. He nurses his beer, and looks up to the muted television screen above the bar, watching for the latest score of some game or another.

Their attention is suddenly drawn to the laughter from a noisy crowd in the middle of the lounge. Thirteen people have pushed tiny bar tables together into a makeshift island that is covered with wine glasses, champagne flutes, flowers, discarded wrapping paper and bows. Someone is celebrating a big birthday, although it's hard to tell which one is the guest of honor. They all seem to be wearing crowns or tiaras.

On the dining room side of the restaurant, a strange energy is starting to grow near the big windows. It's anticipation for something about to happen at table 60. A man in his twenties is sweating profusely, and looking a little too nervous as he waits for his date to choose a dessert. She is oblivious to his nervousness, twirling her long brown hair around her finger as she looks down at the dessert menu. The waiter patiently stands at the ready, waiting for her to choose the chocolate flourless torte. When the waiter leaves, the young man gets down on one knee, and opens a robin egg blue box. The young woman's eyes grow wide and she clasps her hands to her mouth. She starts to cry as he stumbles his way through a heartfelt proposal. Everyone in the restaurant pauses, even the rowdy birthday crowd. What will she say?

"YES!" she shouts, hugging her now-fiancée.

The waiter reappears with two glasses of champagne. Another waiter snaps pictures with the man's phone. Customers clap, offer their congratulations, handshakes and fist bumps, before going back to their dinners.

It's just a regular Friday night at BRAVO!.

The restaurant is the brainchild of two passionately driven, but very different visionaries. Jeff Good is a gregarious, larger-than-life networker who never met a stranger. Dan Blumenthal is a focused and intense culinary creative who thrives on adrenaline and controlled chaos.

BRAVO! has been an institution in Jackson for nearly a quarter of a century, but it never would have been born, if Jeff Good hadn't lost his job.

* * *

Jeff and Dan met during their senior year of high school.

Jeff's father, Stuart, had gotten a job as the Dean of Students at Millsaps College, and moved the family from Salt Lake City. Millsaps is a private, liberal arts college, founded by the Methodist Church and located right in the heart of Jackson.

In 1980, the city of Jackson was at its peak population, and had more people living there than in Salt Lake City proper. But Salt Lake City had been spreading out into the suburbs, and was a huge metropolitan area, much bigger than Central Mississippi. Jackson was also smack in the buckle of the Southern Bible Belt.

When you meet someone from Mississippi, they ask you three questions:

"Where are you from?"

"What do you do?"

And "Where do you go to church?"

That first question is important, because it's not just about where you grew up or your hometown. Mississippians want to know about your family and your "people." Jeff's only people in Mississippi were his mom and dad. He had a much older brother and sister, but they were off starting their lives in another part of the country.

Jackson was a culture shock for Jeff. And going to Murrah High School made it even worse. He stuck out like a sore thumb.

Jeff is tall, standing six feet, five inches, with sandy brown hair, crystal blue eyes and a very prominent nose. In high school, he was also skinny as a rail and wore clothes that are best described as "80s fashion victim". He was an easy target for people to make fun of him.

He was also coming to Murrah High School very late. Most of his fellow students had grown up together, and gone to school with each other for years.

Your "people" aren't just your extended family, it also refers to the people you grew up with at school and at church. Jeff was definitely out of place, and had a hard time making friends.

His mind began to wander one day during a marketing class as he chewed on an ink pen.

"I was sucking on the bottom of my pen and I think it exploded in my mouth."

This caught the attention of Dan Blumenthal, who was also in the class.

"He's got this pen in his mouth, chewing on it and all of the sudden he just starts making all this noise, all this racket and it's obvious he's chewed a hole in his pen. The ink had bled all in his mouth and he's trying to cover it up," Dan laughs.

The teacher asked Jeff what seemed to be the problem. Jeff answered that nothing was wrong. She then asked Jeff to stick out his tongue.

"It was totally blue," Dan laughs.

That sent the entire class into gales of laughter, and the teacher excused Jeff from class to clean himself up.

It was an embarrassing moment that opened the door to a new friendship.

"Dan was nice to me the next day, probably because he wanted to see how dark my tongue was," Jeff said.

From then on, the two were inseparable.

"We just took him under our wing," Dan said.

* * *

Jeff Good is the youngest in his family, while Dan Blumenthal is the oldest in his.

Dan is also tall, but stands in stark contrast to Jeff's fair complexion. Dan has jet-black hair and dark brown eyes that turn nearly black when he's discussing something intense. While Jeff is a transplant, Dan is technically a native. He was born in Jackson.

"Dan for many years would not admit that he was born in Mississippi," Dan's mother, Janice shares. "No one knew it for a long time."

Janice and Buddy Blumenthal are originally from New Jersey and were living in Jackson when Dan was born. Buddy was on his way to becoming a pediatric radiologist and moved his tiny family back to New Jersey for his medical training when Dan was two years old. The family spent a year in New Jersey, two years in Idaho, and four more in Pennsylvania, before returning to Mississippi.

The Blumenthals came back to Jackson in 1972, when Dan was nine. By then, there were three more children. David is three years younger than Dan. Susan and Jon, the twins, came along two years after David.

They too stood out, talking differently than their friends at school.

"Most people still think I'm not indigenous, that I'm a little bit of a Yankee because I don't talk like them," Dan says. "A lot of these people have families that have been here hundreds of years. Their grandfathers and grandfather's father grew up and were born here. But we've been back since 1972. We didn't just move here."

The Blumenthals are a tight-knit family. As the oldest, Dan was in charge of watching after his brothers and sister. He also often played pranks on them. One time he took his sister's Pinocchio doll, covered it in ketchup and put it out in the middle of their street. He told Susan they hit it with the car.

When he was 13 or 14 years old, Dan's parents left him in charge while they went out. Dan took the keys to their station wagon and decided to take everyone for a drive around the neighborhood. He made the twins, Susan and Jon, sit in the back seat and wouldn't turn on the car until everyone put on their seatbelts.

"Susan would always say 'Dan if you dislike us so much and you're always fooling around with us, why do you tell us you're not going anywhere unless we put our seatbelts on?'" Janice smiles. "He was just trying to keep them safe."

Dan had seen first-hand the benefits of seatbelts when he was eleven. He was riding with his father when they got into an accident. The car flipped over into a ditch. Seatbelts saved their lives.

Janice and Buddy were relaxed with the rules around the house, except for one: Dinnertime. No one was excused, not even Buddy with his medical practice.

"Every night we would have dinner at six o'clock," David Blumenthal remembers. "And we all sat down at the table. The only time I can remember any of us were really punished is when we weren't home for dinner. It was the one time of day when we would all get together and we would sit and talk and tell each other about our day."

David makes it sound like an orderly, Norman Rockwell-type of family dinner, but it was more like survival of the loudest.

"When Buddy would come home, there was a lot of noise and commotion," Janice laughs. "Everyone's excited to see Daddy and then they'd start arguing and Buddy would say 'Lock them out! Close the door and let them kill each other outside!'"

Buddy had started dinnertime as a way to connect with his family. His father, Sol, had been a baker in Trenton, New Jersey and kept a schedule that was often opposite to the rest of the family. When they were sitting down to dinner, Sol was already in bed. The family would be asleep when Sol got up at midnight to begin his day at the bakery on Broad Street.

By the time Dan and Jeff began hanging out in high school, the Blumenthal home was the gathering place for teenagers in Northeast Jackson. Dan and Jeff were high school seniors; David was a freshman and the twins were in middle school.

The first time Jeff visited, he was on his best behavior: "I remember going over to Dan's house and playing ping pong on the porch."

It didn't take long for Dan and Jeff to become thick as thieves and get into all sorts of trouble. They started partying, drinking and smoking pot.

That New Year's Eve, Jeff got sick from drinking too much Everclear, a grain alcohol that is 190 proof. He threw up on Dan's mattress, then tried to cover up his "crime" by throwing the mattress out the window, and sleeping in the bathtub. His ruse didn't work, because Dan's bedroom window faced the driveway.

"It wasn't very smart," Buddy Blumenthal laughs. "That was the driveway into the house. First thing you see as you come down the driveway is this mattress lying out under the window of Dan's room. They were in no shape to think rationally."

Dan and Jeff also threw a huge party one weekend when Dan's parents went out of town, even though Janice Blumenthal specifically told them: "no parties".

"We got back and everything was just fine and looked good. And I sat down on the sofa and just put my hand down and felt a beer cap," Janice says.

Turns out, more than 200 people had been at the weekend "kegger" party. The boys thought they had cleaned everything up before Dan's parents returned, but they missed a single, solitary beer cap that got them caught.

Jeff and Dan graduated high school with good grades and went to college, despite all the partying.

Dan chose a college just about as far from Jackson as you could get – the University of California, Santa Cruz, where he considered studying science and following in his dad's footsteps. Even though he was thousands of miles from Jackson, he wasn't completely away from family. He had an uncle who lived in the Bay Area, providing some backup if he needed it.

Dan was smart, and before he officially decided on a major, his father took him to New Orleans for tests at the Johnson O'Connor Research Laboratory.

After the aptitude test, the counselor shared the results and told Dan: "If you want to be pre-med, you can do it. You're smart enough. But you're going to have to work twice as hard as the guy sitting next to you, because that's not where your talents are."

Dan's father also told him not to follow in his footsteps, unless that is what he wanted to do. After that, Dan dropped the sciences and changed his major to Economics.

Stuart Good's position as the Dean at Millsaps meant that Jeff could attend college there at a drastically reduced rate, an 80 percent discount off tuition. But Jeff didn't take college seriously that first year, partying too much and not studying enough.

"When I failed out of college my freshman year, I decided it's time to get a job that pays because I'm going to have to come back to school and hunker down," Jeff said. "I needed to be able to pay my 20 percent of tuition to make it happen."

Jeff had worked in several restaurants as a cashier or host, but he wanted to make more money than minimum wage. His father mentioned a restaurant on The Reservoir called Cock of the Walk. A lot of Millsaps students worked there and made decent money in tips. Jeff went to apply, but the manager asked him if he could wait a month, because they were opening another restaurant right next door, and said Jeff would be perfect for it.

THE BRAVO! WAY

The Other Place was a fine-dining restaurant with beautiful views of sunsets on the water. It was where Jeff first learned to wait tables and began his education about food. This is also where he first learned how to sell.

Jeff brought an incredible amount of energy to each table, describing in great detail the special of the night. He learned early on if he could get customers to order more expensive items, the better his tip would be.

This caught the attention of Abe Dehbozorgi, the general manger at The Other Place. "Mr. Abe" was an older Lebanese man who worked all the time to provide for his family. His face was covered in wrinkles and had an elastic quality to it. When he was frustrated, he would put his hand over his eyes then slowly pull it down his face, stretching the skin out to a near comic expression. Jeff saw him do this many times, and it often was accompanied with Mr. Abe calling him "Jeff Not-So-Good." It wasn't because Jeff had necessarily done something wrong, but instead had caused Mr. Abe to shake his head at Jeff's exuberance.

Mr. Abe had high expectations of everyone, and pushed you to do your best. He was tough but fair, so if you did something wrong, you weren't belittled in front of others – but you might be sent to wait on the "bad" section for your penance.

"He had the ability to just completely engage and have fire in his eyes, but in a very loving way," Jeff recalls. "So if he got upset, he never yelled at anybody. He got excited to make a point about 'this is the way this should be done'. His eyes would light up and his hands curled and he would just get the point across and everyone listened."

Jeff looked up to Mr. Abe, especially how hard the older man worked. Mr. Abe was at the restaurant all the time, from early in the morning until closing. He took a chance on a tall, skinny kid who had never waited tables before – and mentored him, teaching him the tricks of the trade.

When the head waiter left The Other Place, Jeff was the natural replacement.

"Mr. Abe offered me the position to be the head waiter, understanding that I wouldn't be there during the day [because of college classes]," Jeff said. "I was the training guy, and got the best sections."

Jeff even made up "Service By Request" business cards for his new position, and won a Silver Spoon award from the Mississippi Restaurant Association in 1984 – for his "spirit of hospitality."

"I was in Section D all the time, the best section. My section was always full because the hostesses were told to seat me," Jeff shares.

Jeff became a leader at The Other Place, and when Dan came home to visit family during college breaks, Jeff got him a job waiting tables there.

Throughout high school, Dan and Jeff had talked about going into business together. The conversation continued into college, during their down time at The Other Place. They didn't have a specific business in mind but they just knew they wanted to work together. Eventually they began to talk about opening a restaurant and what that would look like.

Jeff was coming into his own on a personal level. People liked his outgoing and friendly nature and he was a magnet for friends at The Other Place. They not only worked hard, but they played hard.

When Jeff got to the point where he had a little money in the bank, he bought a ski boat for $1,400. It barely ran, but that didn't matter to a group of 20-somethings looking to have fun on The Reservoir.

One Sunday afternoon, after working the brunch shift at The Other Place, Jeff and his friends went out to ski for a couple of hours. They skied, drank beer and when they went back to work that evening, they were "hammered" but managed to work their dinner shifts without incident, because they were good at what they did.

Still, the thought of that today doesn't sit very well with Jeff, saying he is ashamed of what they did. It also taught him a valuable lesson about the service industry.

"I've learned so much about what people do in between shifts. Watch your people who do doubles, you never know *how* they're going to come back in."

Even though he worked all the time, and held the respect of the staff, Mr. Abe was let go from The Other Place.

"I don't know why the owners wanted to let him go, but it hurt," Jeff says. "He was like a father figure to me."

Jeff was in shock when the owner brought in someone else to run the business, and he quit out of protest.

His protest didn't last long, because Jeff quickly realized he couldn't make as much money in other jobs as he could at The Other Place, so he apologized and asked for his job back. The new General Manager rehired him, but things weren't going to be the same as they were.

Jeff had been working nonstop when a young woman he had been dating from Ole Miss came to Jackson with her family. They wanted to take Jeff to dinner and he wanted a night off. So he decided to call in sick to work. But this was no ordinary "sick call" – he created an elaborate story about helping his dad who had thrown his back out. While Jeff was calling in sick to work, his father was on the other line to the restaurant – trying to catch Jeff before he started his shift.

That was also the night Miss Mississippi was coming to The Other Place, and Jeff was supposed to be the special waiter for her party. So not only had he lied about being sick, but his absence threw the entire plan for the evening into disarray. Something he would pay for when he returned to work.

"The G.M. harassed me throughout the shift. She was making this long list of things that I was going to have to do to as punishment. All the side work and stuff," Jeff said. "I finished my last table and started doing the work."

This wasn't your typical side work of rolling up silverware, folding napkins or filling up saltshakers. The General Manger had come up with the worst tasks she could think of, like cleaning up the filth underneath all the restaurant sinks.

While Jeff was working on the sinks, she walked up and said: "After you get done with this, go out to the deck. I need you to pick up all the cigarette butts from the cracks in the deck and hose it down."

That was the last straw for Jeff who walked up to her and said: "Screw this, I'm out." He quit The Other Place for the second and final time.

He went on to work at other restaurants, but it wouldn't be long before he was reunited with his mentor. Mr. Abe had found work at a new restaurant called The Lighthouse, which was also on The Reservoir. Mr. Abe hired Jeff as a waiter there, where he remained the rest of his college days.

* * *

Jeff was finishing up his last year of college, when Dan Blumenthal was hitting the real world.

He got his degree in Economics and now it was time to do something with it. That something was a job as a legal assistant at Pillsbury, Madison and Sutro in San Francisco. It was his "safety" job. He really wanted to be an account executive or buyer for Macy's Department Stores, but those positions were competitive, and he didn't get hired.

Dan wore a suit and tie and went to work at the bustling law office, every day. But it didn't take long for him to realize that this legal assistant thing wouldn't be forever.

"While that job was fun, because I was working with smart people my own age, I said to myself: I don't enjoy this. I don't want to be doing this for a career," Dan said.

Something else was drawing his attention – the restaurant scene of the mid 80s in San Francisco.

"Restaurants were cool gathering places. Before that, they were just special occasion places or places to fill your need to eat. They were becoming places of entertainment in the mid-1980s and you had the West Coast Explosion of great chefs. I was in the middle of seeing that. It became a magnet for me."

The cost of living was high in San Francisco, and while Dan lived in a rent-controlled flat with four other guys, he still needed to supplement his income from the law office.

Dan had been working in restaurants since his mother first told him to get a job at the age of 15. He started out as a grill cook at Wendy's in Jackson, and to this day can tell you the not-so-secret ingredient to Wendy's chili. Cooked hamburger patties that aren't fresh enough to be sold as hamburgers, but are still usable, are crumbled up and used as meat in the chili. This was the first time he saw how a restaurant could cut costs by reusing something perfectly fine that might otherwise be thrown out.

Dan worked his way up to nicer and nicer restaurants, eventually joining Jeff at The Other Place during college breaks.

With all the restaurants in San Francisco, and his waiter experience, he knew he wouldn't have trouble finding a place to make extra money. And he might just have fun doing it.

* * *

1986 was a big year for Jeff Good. He was about to graduate from Millsaps with a degree in Business Administration. A month later, he would marry Debbie McGregor.

Debbie met Jeff during a Zoology class their freshman year. That was Jeff's *first* freshman year and he wasn't doing so well in the class, but that's not what caught her attention.

"He was wearing funky clothes. Bad jeans, bad shirts, bad sweaters," Debbie says.

She was drawn to his magnetic personality and saw something special in him.

They went out a few times and eventually started dating exclusively their entire college career – except for a semester when Debbie was a senior. She went to study abroad in Italy, and that's when Jeff briefly dated a young woman from Ole Miss.

Jackson may have thousands of people living there, but it's really just a big small town. Everyone knows your business. College-aged Jeff and Debbie were no exception. Even though Debbie was on another continent, her friends were keeping her informed on what was going on with Jeff. When she returned to Jackson they made up and started dating again, eventually deciding to get married.

Debbie's parents were divorced and her father would go on to remarry four times. She knew when she got married it was going to be a lifetime commitment "no matter what", and that she would have to work through the bad and the good.

"There was something I saw in Jeff that I thought would work, other than just loving him," Debbie says. "It takes more than just love to make a relationship work."

Debbie had graduated and was working as a Latin teacher, while Jeff buckled down and was working hard to finish college. His last three years at Millsaps he had a 4.0 grade point average.

"I watched him through college and he went from being a total screw-up and almost failing out, to then taking an overload of classes, working at a restaurant every night to be able to afford the tuition he had to pay," Debbie says.

The restaurant job also allowed Jeff to buy books, clothes and other necessities, all the while planning to marry Debbie. He also decided it was time to find a "real" job, so he attended a job fair at Millsaps where he only interviewed with two companies.

National Cash Register, NCR, hired him on the spot. Jeff was going to become a computer salesman when he graduated. But it would first mean a year of training.

In May 1986, Jeff graduated from Millsaps. Two months later, he would marry Debbie and head off for six months of computer salesman training in Dayton, Ohio. The time had come for him to leave The Lighthouse, and waiting tables.

At the end of his last shift, he went into the office to hand in his money to Mr. Abe and check out that final time. Jeff took his apron and orange bow tie, and then laid them on the desk. He told Mr. Abe how amazing it has been to work with him, and how much he appreciated him.

"But I've got a real job now," Jeff said.

Mr. Abe looked at Jeff and said: "Jeff Not-So-Good… You'll be back. It's in your blood."

"No, Mr. Abe," Jeff told him. "I've got a real job. I'm getting married. I am done with restaurant life."

Jeff and Debbie got married in July, and instead of taking a honeymoon, they put a down payment on their first house in the Broadmoor neighborhood. A few weeks later, Jeff was off to NCR training in Dayton.

Because he wasn't on the streets selling yet, he made a base salary of $356.15 every week. That's a little more than $18,000 a year. There was no sales commission, and Jeff quickly learned that would not be enough to take care of his new bride, even with her added teacher salary.

Jeff returned from training in Dayton around Valentine's Day of 1987. Not long after, he showed up on the back doorstep of The Lighthouse, asking Mr. Abe if he could pick up a few shifts. Jeff Good was back waiting tables on nights and weekends.

* * *

Dan Blumenthal was also waiting tables in San Francisco. One night, the restaurant he worked for was short on food prep and they threw Dan into the kitchen. He loved it, and it connected to a deep part of him that went back generations.

"The food service business is what my family did. That's what I did as a kid and as a teenager. That's what I liked. It's what I was told I was good at. In San Francisco, I saw that I could be a player in that scene, if I studied and knew the business," Dan said.

He decided to go to culinary school, and called his dad to tell him the news.

"Dad, I'm going back to school."

"That's wonderful! You going to law school?"

"No, I want to go to culinary school," Dan replied.

"[The news] knocked me on my butt because I couldn't believe he was going to do this," Buddy Blumenthal says.

Dan was already thinking about having his own restaurant one day, but in that dream, he wasn't working in the kitchen, or the back of the house.

"I didn't necessarily go to culinary school to be a chef. I went to culinary school to round out my resume to be in the food service business. When you work in a restaurant, if you can't talk to the chef on their level, you don't succeed. You don't get respect. If I didn't get a job as a chef, I still wanted to have the knowledge the chef had," said Dan.

The California Culinary Academy gave Dan the training and background for running a restaurant. He took basic restaurant accounting lessons that he sailed through because of his Economics degree. He learned about different types of food, cooking styles and there was a whole lesson section on wine and liquor. He took to the wine part so well; it became one of his hobbies. He would go on to collect wine and become a connoisseur of it, making connections with vintners at wineries throughout Napa and Sonoma Valleys.

During culinary school, he supported himself by working in the school's restaurant and working at another eatery. A friend got him that job, but Dan butted heads with the chef.

"He wouldn't let me cook on the line. He started me off in prep."

It wasn't the hard work that Dan had a problem with; it was the lack of recognition. In school, he was cooking elaborate dishes, but the chef he worked for only wanted him to do his prep work – chopping up and preparing ingredients for each night's menu items. Dan thought he should have been working on the hot line at the stoves by that point.

Dan spent his days at culinary school learning to run a restaurant's front of the house – where the dining room and bar are located.

"I have the business background. I was going to get the culinary background and then I would take those two and I'd have the power and knowledge to get a job and learn the industry," Dan said. "I was going to succeed come hell or high water. I was going to morph whichever way I needed to morph."

At the California Culinary Academy Bar and Grill, Dan had worked his way up to Assistant Manager and Head Waiter. He was using his Economics degree to do the books and go over restaurant financial numbers, line by line. He also managed a staff of 15 – their scheduling and assignments – along with planning parties and reservations. Dan was only 25 years old.

When he graduated, Dan wanted to work for Larry Mindel at the Spectrum Foods Corporation. Larry was in charge of creating concepts for the restaurant corporation, concepts that didn't feel "corporate". One of those restaurants was Spuntino Italian Express Restaurant. They hired Dan as the Assistant Manager.

Dan kept an eye on expenses while training and supervising the wait staff. He also planned and purchased wine and liquor for the bar. And during his time, he created the concept for a to-go business.

That job lasted a year and a half, when he got the opportunity to become the Manager at Boudin Sourdough French Bread Café, another corporate restaurant. This one was diametrically different than Spuntino. It was as corporate as you can get.

"They would have forms to requisition more forms," Dan says.

They had lured him away with more money and the opportunity to launch a new restaurant concept. But after a year and a half, when the new restaurant didn't materialize, Dan looked elsewhere for a job. He only had to look next door to his neighbor who was the owner/chef of the new restaurant, Café Kati. Dan would become the Manager and Sommelier.

Café Kati was a 50-seat, family-owned fine dining restaurant with a very progressive menu. Dan ran the place for the owner/chef and his wife, trying to keep them on the "straight and narrow."

"The chef was very creative, but very crazy. He would change the menu every week. He would change 60 percent of that menu every week, on Monday or Tuesday," Dan recalls.

That may not sound like a big deal, until you realize everything that goes into a menu change of that magnitude every week. Changing the menu means ordering the ingredients for the new items and making sure they arrive on time. Then, the kitchen staff has to learn all of the new recipes, along with plating, garnishes and side dishes. In the dining room, the wait staff must be able to describe the dishes to a customer, much more involved than the daily special.

"It was crazy to learn it," Dan says. "But the owner-chef was there doing it, so it was able to get done. It was fun and challenging."

That sense of fun didn't last long for him. While he was learning a lot about the restaurant industry, there was something missing. Something was nagging at him.

"After a few years of having adult jobs, I knew that I couldn't work for other people. It was clear that I had enough of a rebellious side to me and just enough knowledge to be dangerous," Dan smiles. "I didn't want to work for other people forever."

* * *

Jeff Good had been doing well working for other people. He went from being a Senior Account Manager at NCR to being the Mississippi Market Manager, in just four years. He covered the area from Tupelo to South Mississippi and was making a living calling on just two medium- to large-sized companies each year to make his sales quota. Things were going well, until 1991, when AT&T purchased NCR. The following year, the company announced it would close Jeff's division and the Jackson office. It seemed every week, fewer and fewer people were in the building, until Jeff was the only salesperson left, and he was forced to also answer the phones in the Jackson office.

When AT&T purchased NCR, they looked through the company for those employees who they felt were worth keeping, and offered them new positions. Jeff wasn't one of the people who was offered a new position right away, nor did they ask him to go through additional management training.

Jeff did talk to several divisions around the company, but every single one of those would mean a move out of state, something neither he nor Debbie wanted.

"I really didn't want to leave," Debbie said. "We would often talk about moving to a larger city because when we traveled, he would ask about living in a larger city and all the things that it affords. I would say we can live in Jackson, live better and have a better lifestyle and be able to travel."

"Bottom line is, we made a decision we're going to stay in Jackson," Jeff said.

That meant looking for a new job. In 1992, he interviewed with WorldCom and even talked to a friend about becoming a commercial real estate agent, but none of that stuck. He had spent so much time positioning himself as a technology expert, he didn't want to leave that industry, so he began talking to a guy about selling two-way paging systems. That manager needed someone who knew computer technology and could sell at the executive level.

Jeff knew relationships were the way to sell those systems, not just showing up and trying to get the purchasing department of a company to buy them. You needed to explain how they would change your business.

"I'm your guy," Jeff told the paging company manager. "And I live right here in Jackson."

It was something he was comfortable with, since he was already doing that level of sales at NCR. This was just a different product.

For several months, Jeff went back and forth with the paging company manager about what a possible position for him would mean. During that time, there wasn't much going on at NCR, so he decided to paint his Belhaven house a lovely shade of Wedgewood Blue. He left early every day to work on it.

At three o'clock one Friday afternoon, Jeff was on the roof of the house. He was painting the chimney when a friend called out to him from the yard.

"What are you doing?" the friend asked.

"I'm painting my house!" Jeff showed him the paintbrush.

"No, I mean what are you doing home? You never come home! Why aren't you at work?"

Jeff came down off the ladder and told his neighbor what had been going on with the job search, and how frustrating it was not knowing if he was going to get the job or not. After hearing the entire story, his friend looked at him and said: "If you want the damned job, you need to ask for the damned job."

It was 4:30 by then, but Jeff was so fired up, he went into the house and called the paging manager, who was still in the office.

"You said you wanted somebody who could close the deal. I'm here to close the deal," Jeff said to the guy. "Can I get this job?"

There was a long pause on the phone, and Jeff got a pit in his stomach.

"I'm getting reassigned," the man said. "We're changing our focus and things are going to be different."

There would be no job after all.

Jeff hung up the phone, devastated. He had put all of his eggs in that basket, and now the basket was gone. He didn't know what else to do, and told Debbie the news. They knew he might possibly get a severance from NCR/AT&T, but he would have to start the job search over.

There was one other person Jeff wanted to talk to, but he would have to wait until midnight to make the call.

Dan Blumenthal had just gotten off work at Café Kati, when the phone rang. It was Jeff. His best friend told him about the bad news he had received hours earlier and how he didn't know what he was going to do next.

Dan shared with Jeff his own disappointment about working for other people, and how unhappy it was making him.

The stories came to an end, and silence filled the line between Jackson, Mississippi and San Francisco, California. Both men shattered the silence by saying, in unison: "Why don't we start a restaurant together?"

* * *

Early the next morning, Jeff was waiting for Debbie to get up. He was bursting to tell her the news.

"Good morning honey, here's your coffee," Jeff passed her a cup. "Guess what? Dan and I are going to open a restaurant."

"Are you crazy?" she asked. "You've lost your mind. How in the hell are we going to live?"

Debbie wasn't the only family member who thought they were crazy. A few days later, Jeff was at a stoplight on Northside Drive in Jackson, when he looked over and saw Janice Blumenthal at the same light.

"Dan and I are going into business! We're going to open a restaurant," Jeff told Janice.

"With whose money?" Janice was skeptical and had many questions. "And where are you going to do this? And how are you going to get Dan to come back?"

"You leave that to me," Jeff said with a smile.

* * *

Getting Dan back to town wouldn't be easy. Jeff wanted to open the restaurant in Jackson, but Dan wasn't about to leave San Francisco on a possibility. So he told Jeff he wouldn't come back to Jackson until the restaurant was 75 percent funded, even though they didn't know what that 75 percent number was just yet.

Getting a loan was out of the question. Even with Dan's experience running restaurants in San Francisco, neither of the 29-year-old men had owned or even opened a restaurant. They would have to get creative for their funding. And that meant they had to do their homework. Dan believed even if they didn't get the restaurant launched, the work that went into creating a viable business plan would be invaluable experience for them.

The first thing they would have to do is decide what sort of restaurant they would open. The first idea wasn't even a restaurant at all. It was a group of espresso carts in Downtown Jackson. They both had seen the gourmet coffee culture explosion in Seattle and wanted to bring that cutting-edge idea to Jackson: coffee carts with some food and pastries.

Jeff got to work outlining the idea in a letter he mailed to Dan. That letter somehow found its way to the attention of Dan's younger brother David, who was in his mid-20s and managing the bar at 400 East Capitol, a fine-dining restaurant in downtown Jackson. The bar was a huge draw for the after work crowd who liked the jazz music and David's cocktails. But he was also looking for his next step. He didn't want to manage a bar forever, and was looking to make his mark.

David met with Jeff and asked to be part of the restaurant Jeff and Dan were opening. Jeff didn't want to get in the way of brothers and told David if it was okay with Dan, it was okay with him. Dan approved and David came onboard.

David nixed the coffee carts idea right away.

"You can't make a living selling coffee," David said. "I mean do the math – two dollars a cup. You've got to sell a thousand cups of coffee a day? It doesn't add up."

It was also too hot in Jackson most of the time for a coffee cart to work. In Seattle, the temperatures were averaging the 60s and 70s for a high, perfect weather for walking around and looking for an expensive coffee. There were only a few weeks out of the year in Jackson where the weather was mild enough for that. Most of the year is spent in boiling summer temperatures in the 90s coupled with high humidity and a lot of bugs and mosquitoes.

"You need to open an Italian restaurant," David said.

"He was the one who came up with the idea of opening something like a Spuntino or Pizza My Heart. That was David's first gift to the business was to say – you guys aren't aiming big enough," Jeff says.

"Dan had worked at Spuntino, and I had been there. I just thought there's not a decent pizza place in Jackson," David explains.

He suggested a wood-fired pizza place, because nobody was doing that in central Mississippi, and pizza just so happened to be one of Dan's specialties.

The men then started working with the concept of an Italian café, with gourmet pizza. Dan developed this idea of a fast-casual café where you would order your food at the counter, take a number, then a waiter would bring your meal to the table.

It was important to get the concept right from the start, because that would drive everything else they would do in the business plan.

"You have to have a concept and the menu. Once you have a concept and the menu, then you can predict what you need in a space," Dan says. "How many seats in the restaurant? If you don't have the number of seats, then your sales numbers aren't right. Everything ties together."

Once you have a menu, a concept and a space – they could get to work on crunching the numbers in the business plan. Dan was putting together the concept while working in San Francisco. David and Jeff were working to find a suitable location in Northeast Jackson.

They wanted a place that was on the east side of Interstate 55, had a lot of customer traffic and good parking. They found two serious contenders: Maywood Mart and Deville Plaza.

The guys didn't just work on one business plan; they had two – to account for the different locations. They were constantly switching between Plan A and Plan B when things would change.

David and Jeff also took a field trip to the restaurant supply store in Jackson. This was 1992, and without an Internet like we know it today, the business plan came together through word processors, fax machines, the U.S. Postal Service and good old-fashioned legwork.

"There was nothing online at the time," David says. "Nowadays you go to a hotel restaurant supply website and you can type in 'Libby glassware' and find out how much a case costs. We went with our list and [they told us] 'It's going to be this much, how much do you need?' We were like damn, this thing's going to be expensive."

David and Jeff's field research included checking out the competition in other Italian restaurants in the area. Neither one of them had a lot of money to go eat at every one of those locations, so they had to piece together what they knew for the competitive analysis. Jeff also spent time going through market research of the demographics in their potential customer base – research that was listed in lengthy printed reports.

One area they were able to save money was to cut their research and printing costs by using Jeff's access to the copier, fax and printer at NCR. Jeff was still working there, managing his remaining accounts and answering the phones while also typing up his part of the business plan, which included the marketing elements.

"I was able to take care of the day's business and I was able to take care of our business, making phone calls," Jeff said.

He didn't just work on his part of the business plan at NCR; he would also work on it at night from home. When he would get a set of pages done, Jeff would then fax them to Dan at Café Kati, where he would grab it off the fax machine before the owners could see what he was up to. Dan wasn't ready to announce he was leaving, because this was still just a fun project he was working on. He wasn't leaving San Francisco just yet.

The project didn't quite feel real. It was an exercise, but one Dan found he was really good at: creating offering documents, spreadsheets, sales projections, profit and loss statements, balance sheets and even a pro forma financial statement. He knew those numbers backwards and forwards. But it wouldn't matter if they couldn't settle on a location. They needed to know how many seats their restaurant would have. Eventually, they decided on Maywood Mart.

Now, all they needed was a name.

They wanted something that would say "Italian" without coming off as a cliché like "Mario's" or "Luigi's". Dan suggested "Cibo y Vino" (Food and Wine), but Jeff and David thought that might be a little too much in Jackson. They were already bringing a revolutionary restaurant concept to town; they didn't want it to be difficult to pronounce too.

They decided to write down names, put them in a hat and draw. Whatever name they drew would be the name of the restaurant.

First name out of the hat: BRAVO!

"BRAVO! will be a special mixture of food, service and atmosphere," the original business plan reads. "The name BRAVO! conveys the primary message of excitement and action, and the name BRAVO! also embraces the Italian theme. BRAVO! is different, yet easy to remember. It relays a sense of cosmopolitan flair without being pretentious."

The big piece to the puzzle was the concept. Dan developed the idea to have a California-inspired restaurant, serving regional Italian cuisine with an emphasis on Northern Italy. There would be appetizers, sandwiches, wood-fired pizzas, pastas and desserts along with other items that the Jackson area had never heard of like: polenta and grilled Portobello mushrooms. The menu had about 25 items on it, all for less than $10.

Dan brought the interior designer to California to show her what he had in mind for the space. He wanted an open-concept restaurant, along with an open kitchen. There would be no separate rooms or heavy curtains separating the dining areas. This would be light and open and airy. It would be painted in colors that reminded you of Tuscany. And the dining room would be completely non-smoking, something unheard of in Mississippi at that time. They had a concept. They had a menu. They had a location. They had a name.

And now, they had a price tag. To pull it off, before they ever served their first plate of food, they would need nearly a half of a million dollars in startup capital. So where were they going to get that sort of money?

Jeff had an idea, and it all started with the ballet.

BRAVO! Caesar Dressing

1 egg, room temperature
1 egg yolk, room temperature
2 tablespoons anchovy paste
4 garlic cloves
1 teaspoon Tabasco or similar hot sauce
1 teaspoon horseradish
1 teaspoon freshly ground black pepper
¼ cup red wine vinegar
1 tablespoon lemon juice
½ tablespoon Worcestershire sauce
2 tablespoons Zatarain's creole mustard
2 cups olive oil
¼ cup grated or shredded Parmesan cheese

Put all ingredients except oil and Parmesan in a food processor. Turn on machine and run for one minute. Slowly add the oil in a stream until it is all incorporated.

The addition of the oil should cause the dressing to thicken and emulsify. Add the Parmesan and blend briefly.

Makes one quart.

Note from Chef Dan Blumenthal: *One of the true backbones to what we do at BRAVO!, this is a recipe that I "borrowed" from my time at Spuntino in San Francisco, where it made many a diner happy in the early 1990s. There is still something special to me about a good Caesar salad, and this makes one of the better ones, in my humble opinion.*

Jeff Good ad Dan Blumenthal in Florida 1992   Photo courtesy Dan Blumenthal

CHAPTER 2

GET TO YES

BRAVO! Management Memo

To: Dan Blumenthal, David Blumenthal
From: Jeff Good
Date: February 8, 1993
Subject: Update on BRAVO!

Here are some things we need to discuss as we complete our business plan:
Staffing:
Now that we have the restaurant floor plan and associated seating capacities determined we need to set our staffing levels. How many kitchen, bar & wait staff? Help, please.
Inventories
As with staffing, what are our new expected requirements for food, liquor and toilet paper?

THE BRAVO! WAY

Take-Out Business

Do we do it? How big/little (emphasized and advertised or just a side line)? Packaging: bows and boxes, butcher paper covered boxes, pizza boxes, Styrofoam, rubber stamp vs. printed, possible use of hot wax with a seal emblem, adequate-sized carrying bags... where do we assemble the orders? Front kitchen, pick up area, wait station? Where do customers pick up? I think the bar is the only logical choice.

Concessions

How much, how little – in what format? Silent vs. overt.

Flavored oils, vinegars, salad dressings, pasta sauces, antipasto, t-shirts, aprons, pizza dough mix, pizza stones, condoms, Torani syrup, etc.

Wines

I want to create a Xeroxed card (paper) for each bottle of wine. This would be a 3x5 form factor. It would have the BRAVO! menu styling as its background and would be the tasting notes for the bottle of wine ordered. Think about it. Dan and David, put together a simple overview of why BRAVO! chose to carry this wine, what it is, what characteristics it has, etc. and the customer takes it home with them! This is major league goodwill. We educate the public and position ourselves as the most knowledgeable and user-friendly restaurant for wine! They take the tasting notes home and want to come back for more!

Methods of Payment – Charge Cards Accepted – House Charges

Here are my thoughts, your input please...we should accept cash, checks, VISA and MasterCard. No AMEX or Diner's Club (too expensive). We should allow our regular customers the opportunity to set up house charge accounts. This will be especially desirable for mass lunch takeout business for offices (if we choose to address this market). Either way, we need to offer house charges, BUT I believe it is against our best interests to worry about billing and collection of said house charges.

THE BRAVO! WAY

So here is my idea: if someone wants to open a house account we take a simple application (name/address/phone #) and TWO CHARGE CARD NUMBERS (VISA & MC). The customer simply signs the bottom of their check, and they're off! We have already pre-approved an appropriate amount through the charge card system and know they are good for the money.

Lynn Green Root

I've been thinking about this one a lot. I think it is a tremendous coup, and a great celebrity tie-in. David and I should meet with Lynn and talk concept. After sharing our findings with Dan, we make a go/no-go decision. If we agree to go with the murals in some form, we get her to prepare a few thumbnail sketches for our swatch board.

PeopleLease vs. Bookkeeper

Spent three hours with PeopleLease and then one with an accountant. We need to talk about this very important issue of payroll, accounts payable and cash control.

Tre Fratelli

I like this name a lot. However, I do not think it gives us any additional market advantage for the same reason we dismissed Il Forno [The Oven]. What if we consider it along with Mangia Bene for our corporate name? It certainly catches the spirit of our partnership – three brothers.

* * *

Jeff and Debbie Good had been volunteers with the Ballet Mississippi in Jackson. Jeff also served on the Board of Directors for the ballet and met longtime members of the community, which included William "Billy" Mounger.

Mounger had graduated from West Point and went on to become a successful banker, oilman and entrepreneur. He had led the Mississippi Republican Party and the National G.O.P., even serving as an advisor to

President Ronald Reagan. He was connected, and he knew how to start a business, using someone else's money.

Jeff told him about BRAVO! and Mounger said he could raise money to start the business by selling shares through a limited partnership. He even offered to get some of his friends from the oil business in a room to hear their pitch.

Dan, Jeff and David worked tirelessly on the presentation—a rudimentary PowerPoint that was twenty-seven slides long. The presentation included their concept, the market overview, detailed operating, marketing and financial plans and how they would structure a limited partnership.

This would be a huge presentation—half a million dollars was on the line—so Dan flew back to Jackson. They stayed up all night, working on and polishing the plan, rehearsing what they would say. Jeff was downing coffee after coffee and running around in a frenzy when Dan said he was shutting down for a power nap. Around 5 a.m., Dan laid down on Jeff's sofa and went to sleep for a half hour. Jeff couldn't sit still so he went over to NCR to print off the presentation for the men they were about to meet.

On March 15, 1993, Dan, Jeff and David met with the Capital City Petroleum Club in a small room and pitched the idea of BRAVO! to five oilmen who were excited to hear about it. They nodded their heads throughout the presentation.

Jim Furrh asked them if they were set on the Maywood Mart location, because he knew of a restaurant that had just closed down. He had been an original investor in The Sundancer Restaurant when it opened in 1977, and always had an affinity for the place. The BRAVO! team said they would give it a look.

At the end, the oilmen took a straw poll—who was interested? Jim Furrh and Billy Mounger were. Could this be the big payday they were hoping for?

"I'll do $10,000," Mounger said.

"So will I," Furrh agreed.

One oilman wanted to think about it, the others weren't interested.

Jeff, Dan and David all did the math in their heads, that's only $20,000—a long way off from the half million dollars they needed. They were happy to get that, but felt like a truck had hit them. They were exhausted, coming off of an adrenaline rush, and felt a little let down.

Still, it was good to have Dan back in Jackson, back home, even if it was just for a few days. Jeff and Debbie invited everyone over to their house. Dan, David and his girlfriend and the youngest Blumenthal brother, Jon, all joined in the impromptu party. They put on music, made food and opened wine, then started talking about the next steps.

"This is going to be harder than we thought," Jeff said. "We're going to have to sell a lot of those limited partnerships."

Jeff knew they would get questions about their ability to run a restaurant and what did it mean their restaurant would be "Italian." Olive Garden was coming to Jackson and they wanted to make sure they weren't being compared to that restaurant chain or any other Italian-style restaurant in the area.

Jeff looked around at his house, at the people and the food and the wine glasses. He realized they would have to find dozens more people to invest $10,000 each to make their goal. And he also knew they would be hard-pressed to find people willing to part with ten grand on the *idea* of a restaurant, they would need tangible proof of concept, of what the restaurant would offer. And that proof would be in the proverbial pudding. Or risotto as the case may be.

* * *

The Sundancer Restaurant was located in Highland Village. It was a location David knew well; he waited tables at The Sundancer when he was in high school.

"I worked for Bill Latham and Al Roberts who at the time owned The Sundancer," David says. "The Sundancer had historically been one of the best restaurants in Jackson. They did tableside Caesar salad. They did flambé Bananas Foster and Steak Diane."

The Sundancer was a very pricey restaurant where the waiters wore tuxedo shirts, bow ties and cummerbunds. It received awards for the cuisine and wine list, but Latham and Roberts sold it in 1988. The restaurant changed hands many times during its history and the last owner "sundowned" it, closing it permanently.

It was now an empty space in Highland Village, which had about 40 other businesses, but only three of them were restaurants: Highland Grill, Old Tyme Deli, and Shoney's.

David and Jeff stepped through the heavy custom-carved wooden front doors of The Sundancer and walked into a world that was frozen in time, back to the last night it was open, just a few weeks prior. The hostess stand with its mirrored front and antler-head motif, the tables with their iron bases and wood tops surrounded by rattan chairs, heavy wooden beams overhead gave the dining room a claustrophobic feel. There was a custom bar with an elephant head brass rail and twenty pairs of brass antlers mounted above it. Animal heads and antlers were hung on the walls, all throughout the space, making you wonder if it was a restaurant or a long-lost hunting camp.

But that was all just on the surface. Decorating that could be changed.

What The Sundancer had that the Maywood Mart location didn't have, was that it was already an existing restaurant space. Its 5,379 square feet already had the footprint for a kitchen, a 110-seat dining room with 40 additional seats in the cocktail lounge and bar. This would cut down on their initial construction costs.

At Maywood Mart, they would have to build that from scratch. Highland Village was located on Northside Drive, Exit 100, right off of Interstate 55, which meant plenty of customer traffic, and there were plenty of parking spaces.

It was perfect.

* * *

THE BRAVO! WAY

March 27, 1993
Dear Gentlemen:
A brief update regarding BRAVO!

We have spent the last week working with the management of Highland Village concerning the possibility of refitting Sundancer for the BRAVO! concept. Our research includes a complete contractor's bid for comprehensive remodeling of the space.

You will be pleased to learn that we will be able to build-out BRAVO! for $396,920, including all construction, equipment, furniture, finishes, inventories and $50,000 in working capital allowance.

The Sundancer space has been empty for two weeks, and already a total of three restaurants have shown interest. We think this location is perfect for our concept, and the Highland Village management agrees. As you can see from the drastic reduction in startup costs, there is a tremendous attraction to securing this location. Less up front capital means a quicker payback and better return to our investors. We do not want to let this most significant opportunity slip through our fingers.

Attached, please find an updated menu along with a representative list of possible entrees we will feature. Remember, the BRAVO! concept utilizes a changing menu, which means that we will be able to constantly update and add exciting dishes at will. In addition, you will find a revised Startup Expenses-Beginning Balances spreadsheet, which details the specific costs to open. A five-year financial statement is also included, which will allow you to confirm that our new, lower costs will indeed meet your investment requirements.

The task at hand is to secure your sincere interest and support so we can move forward quickly.

Respectfully,
Jeff E. Good
-Follow-up letter to the oilmen after the first meeting.

* * *

With The Sundancer in place as the location, they now knew the exact number they would have to reach in investments: $440,000. If they sold shares worth $10,000, they would need 44 investors.

Jeff's restaurant experience had all been in the Jackson, Mississippi area. His fine dining background had been pretty straightforward, but the menu that Dan was creating was new to Jeff. He knew if he was still trying to understand it, potential investors would be confused too.

"I realized we needed to do something that was tangible. We need to show people what the food *was* because that was the big thing," Jeff says.

They decided showcasing the BRAVO! food to potential investors would be the best way to show proof of concept. Dan had to go back to California, but shared his recipes with David – who would cook the food and curate the wine during weekly cocktail parties for investors.

Jeff and Debbie planned to host weekly cocktail parties at their two-bedroom home in Belhaven and invite a dozen people at a time to sample food and wine. When people had their fill, Jeff and David would take the floor and make the pitch.

But nothing could happen until they finished the Private Placement Memorandum, or offering document. They had hired attorney T. Jackson Lyons to put together the legal requirements of an offering document that allows you to solicit money for your business.

The one for BRAVO! included the business plan, Investor Suitability Questionnaire, Subscription Agreement and the Agreement of Limited Partnership.

"We were so conservative about how we're going to do this business, that we only sold to people who had wealth," Jeff said. "If you sold to somebody who is like grandma on her Social Security check, who gives us money because 'he's such a precious boy,' and we failed, we would damage her, but she could have legal action against us because she was not a suitable investor for a high risk investment."

The Investor Suitability Questionnaire had three parts. In part one, there were questions about your current investments, your job history and educational background.

Part two was the biggest piece of the questionnaire: making sure people were "accredited investors". People, corporations or trusts with a substantial net worth or income qualify as "accredited investors". They were looking for individuals with a net worth of more than a million dollars, or a combined income with a spouse of $300,000 or an individual income of $200,000.

Corporations or partnerships could also invest if they had assets in excess of five million dollars, or the equity owners met the individual income requirements, or they were a registered investment company.

Part three centered on your knowledge of and experience with investments. Even though Jeff and Dan knew BRAVO! would be a success from the beginning, they had to make sure they got to "yes" the right way.

"I didn't want to have anybody who had a whole bunch of money in the business. That's why we sold small shares of $10,000," Jeff said.

He was about to reach out to hundreds of people he had met over the years, asking them to invest in BRAVO!. If the restaurant failed, Jeff would see these people around town and he wanted to be able to look them in the eye, knowing they did everything to ensure people were aware of the investment risks.

"I didn't want to be looking at my shoes while I was in Kroger."

Explanations of this risky investment are found all throughout the document.

Section 11 of the Subscription Agreement reads:

The undersigned represents, warrants and agrees that he, she or it has been made fully aware that the Partnership has no operating experience, that no federal or state securities regulatory agency has passed on the merits of this investment, that there is a significant risk of loss, that an investment in the Partnership is illiquid and the investor may bear the economic risk of this investment for a significant period...

Basically – three guys with no experience of opening a restaurant are asking for you to invest your money and you agree that it's a high-risk investment, but you want to invest anyway.

The 113-page business plan starts off with seven pages of "Risk Factors" that included phrases like:

BRAVO! will be an unproven "product" in that it has neither operational nor financial history for investors to assess.

The limited partnership will create, own and operate only one business property, BRAVO!

Restaurant businesses are not easily sold on the open market.

The restaurant business has historically one of the highest failure rates of any type of business.

The three shareholders of the General Partner [Jeff Good, Dan Blumenthal, David Blumenthal] *have never worked together as operators of a restaurant before.*

"Our business plan had seven pages of 'we're running with scissors, don't give us any money,'" Jeff laughs about it now.

But they did know what they were doing. Dan, David and Jeff all had degrees in business and Dan's restaurant management experience gave them a head start, especially with the financials, which was a big chunk of the business plan. They laid out sales projections for the first five years. The costs of running the business were spelled out right down to the prices of forks and uniform shrinkage. There was an estimated return on investments, and how they planned to pay off the investors within five years.

When the offering document was ready to print, they took it to an accounting firm to certify their numbers. Dan, Jeff and David had spent nearly a year on this plan, and the reaction from the accountants wasn't what they expected.

"We went in front of the accountants with our numbers. They laughed at us and said: 'You know it sounds like a great idea, but you're probably going to fail,'" Dan says.

In July 1993: the accountants signed off on their numbers, without making a single change.

"They told us we'd fail, then they charged us five thousand dollars to do nothing," Dan said.

Billy Mounger was impressed with the offering document and dropped a check in the mail the day he got it. His $10,000 arrived the next day. Not long after came the $10,000 check from Jim Furrh. BRAVO! had its first two investors, now they only needed 42 more.

* * *

Dear xx:

Dan Blumenthal asked me to drop you a line with some details regarding our business venture: BRAVO!. The result of eleven months of research and planning, BRAVO! embodies a number of unique and differentiating qualities, which should ensure immediate and long-lasting acceptance in the Jackson dining marketplace.

Our intent is to bring a new dining phenomena to Jackson: a metropolitan Italian trattoria serving exceptional and creative Italian fare, prepared in authentic style using ingredients and cooking implements true to the form, served in a visually stimulating, exceptionally outfitted environment at very reasonable prices ($10 and below). An exposed kitchen is the centerpiece of activity, with all food prepared in plain view. The menu is varied, with imaginative pastas, flavorful appetizers, generous focaccia bread sandwiches, innovative salads and gourmet pizzas cooked in a wood-fired oven.

We have a great team built, ready for a winning performance. Dan Blumenthal is my best friend from high school. He is a classically trained chef with a rich and varied background of restaurant experience, especially within the market niche we are bringing forward. David Blumenthal, Dan's younger brother, is the bar manager at 400 E. Capitol, with a strong knowledge of wine and the knowhow to run and control a large, upscale bar operation.

Enclosed, please find some brief outtakes from our offering document and business plan. The complete prospectus includes market research information, menus, design and concept descriptions, five years of financial projections, partnership agreement contracts, etc. and is available upon request.

Enclosed, you will also find reprints from Gourmet Magazine, which review two restaurants Dan has managed in San Francisco, including Spuntino, the high-tech Italian café from which Dan gained significant competence in the trattoria concept.

We would like to invite you to my home for a sampling of the few items from the BRAVO! menu, and for a brief overview of the BRAVO! concept, theme and financials. The evening begins at 7:00 p.m. with a cocktail buffet and wine service, and finishes at 9:00 p.m. with dessert and coffee. I'm sure you will find the format to be most enjoyable and productive.

We have two dates scheduled: Tuesday and Thursday.

We thank you in advance for your consideration. Please expect a telephone call soon to query your interest. In the meantime, if I may answer any questions, please feel free to contact me.

Sincerely,

Jeff E. Good

[Letter to potential investor, inviting them to an upcoming cocktail party].

* * *

The last bell rang, signaling the end of the school day for Debbie Good. She had just enough time to stop at Kroger for some flowers on the way home.

David Blumenthal was headed to Old Tyme Deli to buy special ingredients for tonight's potential investor cocktail party.

At four o'clock, he arrived at the Good home just as Debbie was finishing her final walk-through of the house, straightening pillows, touching up the bathrooms for guests, and making sure the place was spotless.

David got started on the food prep and making that night's food. There would be two different types of pizzas, bruschetta for an appetizer, risotto, and tonight there would be profiteroles, tiny cream puffs, for dessert. Everything would be made from scratch, and David had three hours to get everything done.

Jeff was going over the presentation one more time with their attorney Jack Lyons. He was there to make sure they followed the "Blue Sky Laws", federal and state regulations that protect investors from fraud.

"He insisted on coming to each and every cocktail party so he could be in the room to ensure that laws were followed and disclosures were made," Jeff said.

Just after six o'clock, people began arriving for the party. Two of those first guests were Janice and Buddy Blumenthal, who wouldn't have missed this for anything. Eventually a dozen more people joined them: filling the Good home, eating hors d'oeuvres, drinking wine and laughing.

"The mood was festive, because Dave and Jeff plied everybody with lots of wine," Buddy Blumenthal says. "Everybody got to meet each other."

After the food, everyone settled down in the living room to hear the pitch. This was Jeff's moment, and he was on.

"Jeff is so full of energy. He's a salesman and very positive," Janice says.

Jeff is a natural-born salesman. He's full of energy and when he is in his element, his eyes light up and practically sparkle. His smile is infectious and you just feel comfortable around him. His easy-going manner had been a benefit when waiting tables and while selling computers, and it would be the way they would get to yes for BRAVO!

For every presentation, he brought that same energy and self-effacing humor. He would work his way through the presentation, engaging with every single person in the room, talking directly to them. He wasn't just selling them on the concept; he was also making sure he laid particular legal groundwork with potential limited partners.

"We're only looking for sophisticated investors," Jeff would say. This was code for – those individuals who would meet the Investor Suitability standards.

His positive energy is contagious and you find saying "no" to Jeff Good is hard to do. Some people did say no. They just weren't ready for this risky of an investment.

"Their ideas were good. Their numbers were good," Buddy said. "Their business plan would have passed muster with virtually anyone it was that good. But the concept was so foreign to Jackson that they had to feed people in order to convince them that there's a market for this in Jackson."

Janice didn't need to be convinced. She walked in the door ready to say yes and wrote a check that very night, making her the first investor from the cocktail parties.

"I had to as a mother and a parent, I believed in those guys," she said.

When the party came to an end, Jeff handed every potential investor a hand-numbered copy of the offering document.

"That document stood for us when you were back in your office after having dinner and a glass of wine," Jeff says. "I was going to call you two days after the party and follow up."

People who were ready to invest would need to fill out the Subscription Agreement and Investor Suitability Questionnaire and give those to Jeff along with their $10,000 check. Jeff would review each one to make sure people met the investment requirements; otherwise he would reject their offer. Because Jeff did a lot of pre-vetting on the front end at the parties, none of the people who wrote him a check after the parties was rejected as an investor.

Around ten o'clock, the last guest left. Debbie, Jeff and David began cleaning up the house and kitchen. Debbie carefully wrapped up the leftovers from the party and placed them in the refrigerator. The supplies for the cocktail parties were coming out of Jeff and Debbie's budget.

"We'd have to buy all the groceries, all the wine, all of this not really knowing if all of this was going to come to fruition," Debbie shares. "Whatever people didn't eat, this is what we ate for the rest of the week. This was all I ate for months!"

The first few parties were fun, especially when people said yes and wrote a check. Every week they hosted at least one cocktail party, often two, looking to get to that magic number of 44 investors. But in those groups of 12 people each week, you might only have one or two who said yes. Raising the money was slow going, and it was starting to take a toll.

"Months of washing all the napkins, all the linens, ironing them and cleaning the kitchen every time. And cleaning the house and keeping it spotless," Debbie listed off everything she would do before, during and after the parties. "Thank goodness we didn't have children then."

This was in addition to her full-time job as a teacher, which started very early in the morning. Jeff wanted her to stay for the presentation each night, but eventually she would start ducking out and head into the kitchen to clean up. She had to get to bed.

In between the parties and work, Debbie would also go to the grocery store to buy the regular ingredients for menu items, and then head to the liquor store for the wine.

"There was a stretch there where it was a lot of work," David Blumenthal adds. "It was an exciting time and I didn't mind the cooking, but it got a little crazy."

One afternoon, Jeff called David to talk about the parties scheduled for the week ahead. Even Jeff was feeling the grind of being "on" all the time, trying to raise money for the restaurant, but he was determined to get to 44.

"We've got another one on Thursday," Jeff said.

David let out a heavy sigh on the other end of the line.

"Is this ever going to end?" David asked.

"Yes!" Jeff raised his voice, the tone getting higher and higher with each sentence. "It's going to end when it's done! When we're done! We're not going to stop until it's done!"

To make matters worse for David, one day he got a phone call from someone he worked with at 400 East Capitol. The owner was closing the place down, for good.

"They just basically shut the doors one day and that was it, but it just happened to work out for me," David says. "Timing-wise I could survive at the time going through that process. It was a difficult time financially, but I didn't have any kids and I wasn't married."

David was now officially unemployed. Jeff was about to lose his job. It became more important than ever to get all of the investors in place, so they could get BRAVO! open.

* * *

Within two days of each cocktail party, Jeff Good would be on the phone, following up with potential investors. He was a salesman who knew you had to be persistent to get your "yes". And even those who said no to him, he would ask for one more thing – a referral to someone else who might be interested in the investment opportunity.

Nowadays, if you have a meeting with Jeff Good, you have to factor in "Good Time" – an extra 20 minutes on either side of your meeting. Sometimes Jeff is late because a person who needs help or wants to ask him a question holds him up at his previous meeting. Other times, especially if you're meeting at one of his restaurants, it will take him 20 minutes to just cross the room to get to you. People stop him at every step, like he's a Beatle or something.

This was not the case 25 years ago.

People would see Jeff Good coming into a building and they would quickly walk, or run, in the opposite direction. That's because he would pitch BRAVO! to anyone who would listen. There were Amway salesmen and Jehovah's Witnesses who were more popular than he was.

So when a complete stranger called him at NCR to ask about the investment, Jeff was surprised and ecstatic. People were responding to his requests for leads!

"Glad you called, let me tell you about BRAVO!," Jeff was standing at his desk and started pacing back and forth.

The stranger was calling from Florida and had heard about their investment opportunity, but he had some questions.

"Here's what I need to know," the man cut Jeff off. "How big is your board of directors gonna' be? Who's going to be your treasurer?"

"Well, we're not setting this up as a corporation," Jeff said. "You haven't had a chance to read our prospectus yet. We're forming a limited partnership; the investors in the limited partnership will be passive investors. My two partners and I are going to manage it as the general partn…"

"You know, I'm not interested in something like that," the man cut Jeff off again. "All those doctors and dentists they want to invest in these things. They don't know anything about money. They don't understand how expensive it is to run a restaurant. They don't understand how much it costs to buy linen each day from the linen service. They don't know how expensive food is. They don't understand when the cooler goes down, and you have thousands of dollars in fish in there and it goes bad. They don't understand that you gotta' buy all that again. That's why you need somebody like me to manage the checkbook, because I understand how expensive things are."

Jeff is confused and still not understanding exactly what this guy is getting at.

"My partner has run restaurants in San Francisco and I think he'll understand…" Jeff started.

"No, no, no, you don't understand how this works," the man kept cutting him off. "I want to invest and I want to invest half of the money, how much are you trying to raise anyway?"

"Well sir, in our prospectus, which I need to mail to you for review, we're selling 44 shares of $10,000 units," Jeff explained.

"So, I'll give you $225,000 and I'll have 51 percent and I'll have a seat on the board of directors and I'll be the Treasurer," the man said.

Jeff's heart started beating faster, not because he's this close to raising half of the needed capital for BRAVO! He realized something is amiss. There's a nefarious vibe from this man, who still hasn't said his name, and now Jeff is worried that this shady character knows where he works. Possibly where he lives.

"We're interested in selling a single share of 44 to have a broad group of investors who then eat with us, and create a customer base," Jeff began backing out of the conversation. "We're not looking for one investor to buy everything."

"I'm offering half your deal, and you're not going to take it?" the guy on the other line was incredulous.

"No sir, that's now how we're going to do this," Jeff said. "That's not our plan."

That was the end of the conversation. After they hung up, Jeff's heart would continue to beat a rapid pace for a long time as he wondered if he would find a horse's head on his doorstep, or worse.

* * *

Between Jeff's contacts and their referrals, he eventually prospected 750 people, inviting them to his cocktail parties. Of those 750, 250 people said yes to showing up for the food, wine and The Pitch.

"One of my strongest memories of doing those dinners are the people getting excited about it and willing to part with their money," David says. "There were obviously people who were involved with it, no matter what – like my parents!"

There were the people who were a little more skeptical. Those who knew Jeff, David or Dan and came to hear The Pitch, but would question them about their experience with something like this.

Then, they would try the food and realize there wasn't anything like it in the Jackson market, and they wanted in.

In the fall of 1993, after months of parties, they reached the magic 75 percent.

Jeff called Dan to bring him home.

"I was kind of shocked when he said 'we've got 75 percent of the money, you have to come back,'" Dan says. "I don't think I ever worried about him getting the money. I just knew it would take a while to do. But I knew that he could do it."

Debbie had a different reaction.

"It got really real, and it was scary," she says. "It was the time when I knew Jeff was actually going to quit. He was going to have six months of a paycheck and if things weren't open by then, we'd go without – everything."

Dan got ready to pack up and leave his life in San Francisco, including the sweet rent-controlled apartment. It also meant a move for the guys living with him, because the lease was under Dan's name. David went to California to help his big brother move home.

While they were still more than a hundred thousand dollars away from their goal, Highland Village was getting antsy about The Sundancer location. Other restaurateurs were interested in the spot, and if BRAVO! wanted it, they better do something about it.

"We were getting pressure from Highland Village to execute the letter of intent. So we went ahead and signed the lease, making the commitment. That gave us the right to gain access to that space," Jeff says.

And with that, came all the restaurant décor left behind by the last owner of The Sundancer. The brass bar, the animal heads that were everywhere, the chairs, the tables, even the forks and glasses. Everything. The landlord told Team BRAVO! that they could have everything in the space. It was theirs to do with as they pleased. And it definitely pleased Jeff because he had an idea.

Jeff brought in the top auctioneer in Jackson, Larry McCool, to see about getting rid of everything. Auctioning off anything that wasn't nailed down, and maybe a few things that were. The auction would raise some of the money needed to open BRAVO!

"Larry was amazing. He led us through what to do, told us to get your bar set up and get some wine in there, get people's spirits up," Jeff says. "We're going to sell everything that was left in The Sundancer."

On October 20, 1993, Jeff opened up The Sundancer to a big party. He invited current investors and potential investors, and anyone who was curious about what was going on in the space.

As a result, more than 120 people packed into the place, looking though the items, drinking their wine and cocktails. When the auction finally got underway, people started a bidding frenzy. They bought the tables. They bought the chairs. They bought the animal heads. They bought sinks and vacuums.

Janice and Buddy Blumenthal bought the two ornately carved front doors from the Sundancer.

The stuff that was nailed down? That was on the auction block too.

A carpenter came to Jeff and said: "I'll buy all of your woodwork from you, but I'm not going to pay you. I'm going to remove it all. I'll demo it and take it."

Jeff thought that was a good deal, and told him "sold!" If the carpenter hadn't taken the woodwork out, their construction team was going to have to remove it anyway, costing money – so the deal saved them in construction costs.

The huge wooden beams overhead – sold.

The baby grand piano – sold.

At the end of the night, they had sold a few more limited partnership shares and brought in $30,000 from the auction.

Within days, The Sundancer would be stripped almost bare. No more tables and chairs. The woodwork was removed. There were wires and can lights sticking out of the ceiling. You could see spots on the walls, where pictures or animal heads had been, but now was just a dark spot on the paint or wallpaper.

Before they got to work fixing it up into BRAVO! they had to throw one more party. And Jeff had a very important letter to fax to his boss. It was time to quit.

Jeff had been in two worlds for months. Working at NCR, waiting for his job to be eliminated, and preparing for his future by raising money to open BRAVO!

In the days after the auction, Jeff decided it was high time to quit his sales job at NCR.

"The sweetest day was the day that I faxed the resignation letter in to my boss. He called me back and he had no idea I was planning to open a restaurant."

"Jeff, there's going to be a reduction in force at the end of the year, you might want to be part of that," the boss told him.

"What does that mean?" Jeff asked.

"I don't think you want to resign right now. I think you want to wait."

Jeff told him he would wait, and his boss threw out the resignation letter. The end of the year was only six weeks away. Jeff could wait a little longer.

* * *

**The furniture is gone,
And the zebra head too,
Yes, my friends,
There's but one thing to do…
Say goodbye to the old
And hello to the new;
Saturday night at seven
We have an invitation for you!
Saturday, October 30
Sundancer Restaurant
7:00 p.m.
Exorcism of The Sundancer ghosts and Welcome Back Party for Chef Dan Blumenthal
Casual Dress!**
[Handwritten invitation to The Exorcism Party]

* * *

During the auction, people were milling about in The Sundancer space, excited for a new restaurant. But there were plenty of skeptics in the crowd that night. What were these guys going to be able to do that previous Sundancer owners couldn't? Wasn't this just going to be another version of The Sundancer?

Jeff decided they would hold another party, the night before Halloween.

An exorcism.

"We needed help because the number one thing that's happening is people saying 'you're going to keep The Sundancer the same! It's failed five times!' We wanted to physically show people that it was not going to be the same," Jeff said.

They invited back the same people who attended the auction, and a few more. Those people hadn't seen the space decimated yet. The invitations were hand-written on old Sundancer order forms.

Jeff wasn't going to do this party half-assed, either. Never mind the fact that there were few places to sit and there was no heat in the restaurant. He again set up the bar and they brought in food.

Two of Jeff's friends created a parody song that was a mashup of "The Beverly Hillbillies" and the "12 Days of Christmas" that was titled "On Any Day at Sundancer."

The highlight of the evening was Jeff blessing the place with dried pasta.

"We broke a bottle of champagne on the old fireplace and I had a little speech that we now claim this as our own. We released the evil spirits of The Sundancer," Jeff said.

Dan and David had made it back to Jackson in time for the party and joined the 75 other partygoers on that Saturday night.

That night, they sold the final shares of BRAVO!

The exorcism, or business blessing, appeared to be working.

* * *

With all of the money coming in, and BRAVO! now on track to really open, the guys needed to hire a bookkeeper.

Linda Kay Russell and her husband had been living in Chicago, but decided to return to Jackson. They just had their first child and Linda Kay was looking to get back to work as a Certified Public Accountant.

One evening they ran into a friend who told Linda Kay about Jeff Good and Dan Blumenthal who were about to open a restaurant. They needed a full-time bookkeeper.

"I'm a CPA, I can do that part-time," Linda Kay told him with a laugh.

A few days later, Linda Kay found herself sitting across the table from Jeff and Dan at the Highland Grill in Highland Village. She ate her salad while an incredibly animated Jeff talked about the BRAVO! concept, selling her on the job. Dan focused on the numbers, and was very serious about their need for a bookkeeper to keep the cash under control.

Linda Kay was impressed and it didn't even cross her mind that the restaurant might not make it, despite the odds stacked against them.

"They were taking on me who knew very little about restaurants. I had audited banks in Chicago. I had appraised mobile home parks. I had no experience with a restaurant and you just don't realize how often they fail and how complicated they are," Linda Kay said.

Dan and Jeff liked her and hired her, preparing for her to start in January.

"She was the first person we hired because we had to set up the books and the processes and all that stuff, so she was on board," Jeff said.

They wanted to make Linda Kay feel at home, so they set up a tiny office for her in the back, right next to the beer cooler. The same day Jeff painted the bathrooms, he painted Linda Kay's office. He was using a sprayer, and arguably got more paint on himself and in his eyes, than he did on the walls.

They also needed to hook up a computer for their new bookkeeper, who planned to work part-time in the beginning. Jeff spent hours trying to use telephone wire to make a network in the restaurant, which didn't work.

By now, it was getting close to Christmas and there was a big change coming for Jeff. The day he had finally waited for and worried about was here – he was losing his job. The reduction in force at NCR meant layoffs, but it also meant a severance and unemployment money starting in January.

Despite the bad news, the company went ahead with their Christmas party at the Steak 'N Ale for 20 people, employees and their spouses.

Jeff would play Santa Claus and had a surprise for his co-workers.

"I put on a Santa suit and I came to the party. I had gone into the kitchen and gotten a pan and some dried pasta," Jeff remembers. "I did this little thing where I shook the pasta and made the announcement to everybody I worked with that we were going to open a restaurant."

It was a huge weight off of Jeff's shoulders.

"I think one person in the entire place suspected something, but I was able to break down all those barriers and tell everybody the honest truth of what I was doing."

He wasn't just starting a restaurant either. He would have skin in the game. There are actually 45 shares of BRAVO! – the 44 they sold to the investors and number 45, which was split between Jeff, Dan and David. They would become the General Partner as the Mangia Bene Restaurant Management Group, a for-profit corporation.

They each put in $3,333.33, but that left them one cent away from the rounded off number on share price that the State of Mississippi requires for corporations, so Jeff put in an extra penny – making him the President of Mangia Bene. The guys felt he was the natural person for the job, since he had managed the majority of the paperwork for getting the business started.

* * *

Dan also had a big moment at the end of 1993. He was inducted into the Chaîne des Rôtisseurs. It's the "oldest and largest food and wine society in the world," founded in Paris in the 13th century and there had never been a chapter in Mississippi. Being inducted was a huge honor that would extend to the restaurant.

For the induction, Team BRAVO! would travel to the Northwood Country Club in Meridian to present a wine dinner for the packed house, including the 28 inductees from the state of Mississippi. The theme was "A Celebration of Tuscany," a nod to the BRAVO! concept, and received rave reviews from the international society.

There were also three Chaîne des Rôtisseurs plaques handed out that night, the first ever to adorn businesses in Mississippi. One of those went to BRAVO! and is still mounted outside the restaurant to this day. If you've ever visited in the last quarter of a century, you've probably walked right past it and didn't even notice.

1993 ended on a high note as BRAVO! moved forward, but the hard work was still ahead of them.

* * *

By the start of 1994, the space formerly known as The Sundancer had been completely cleaned out. The bar was gone. The fireplace. Everything was out and BRAVO! began to take shape.

One of the first orders of business was the huge oven Dan ordered from Italy. This is the wood-fired oven that would be a centerpiece for the back of the restaurant and where pizzas would be made. The oven was three thousand pounds and needed a cinderblock foundation to support it.

The day it arrived, the delivery drivers took it off the truck and looked at the back door of the restaurant, the one that opened into the kitchen. They wouldn't be able to bring the oven in that way, because the equipment was too big. The only other option was to drive it through the front doors, but that was tricky.

BRAVO! is located on the second level of Highland Village, which you don't always realize until you walk down the walkway, which is more like a bridge, to the front doors. The kitchen part of BRAVO! sits on the ground, adjacent to the back parking lot of Highland Village. The lounge area on the far side of the restaurant is on the second level of the shopping center. And in between is the dining room, which is on the same bridge as the walkway, spanning a driveway in the lower parking lot.

Buddy Blumenthal, Dan, David, Jeff and the entire construction team stopped and watched as the delivery guys suspended the oven by chains from a forklift, then drove it slowly down the walkway.

"As they came over that bridge, I was walking behind and you feel the bridge swaying [back and forth under the weight]," Buddy said.

The workers got the oven in through the front doors, inside the lounge area, then turned to take it straight back to the kitchen. When the driver got to the middle of the dining room, he joked: "I'm starting to go uphill here!"

Within a few more minutes, he was back on the solid "ground" of the kitchen area, and they were able to maneuver the oven in place.

Lesley Tolar was among those watching this oven drama unfold in the restaurant. She was sitting at a card table, waiting for her job interview.

* * *

Lesley had waited tables and bartended while she attended college at Millsaps, but when she graduated she was under a huge amount of pressure from her parents to get a "real" job.

"I didn't really know what to do with my Millsaps history degree with a French minor and an Art History minor," Lesley says. "I thought maybe I should just go into retail and get a management position."

She was hired as a manager for a retail-clothing store in the mall, making an "awful salary" but she had insurance. She hated every minute of it, especially when she remembered how much money she made bartending, and 400 East Capitol was hiring.

Lesley worked there when David Blumenthal was the bar manager and the happy hour was the draw in downtown Jackson.

"It was way before its time. We had a banging happy hour and then at seven o'clock, everybody left," she says.

In 1993, during their down time, David would tell his bartenders about the restaurant he was about to open with his brother and a high school friend.

"We're like 'Okay cool! We're all going to work there!'" Lesley recalls.

But time went by, and 400 East Capitol closed, so Lesley had to find another job and went to work at George Street.

One afternoon in January 1994, the phone rang at George Street. David was calling for Lesley.

"Hey Les," David said. "Listen, you want to come down here and fill out an application? You know we're opening that restaurant!"

"You really opening the restaurant?" Lesley asked.

"Yeah, it's in Highland Village, you know where The Sundancer was?"

Lesley didn't know where The Sundancer was, because she had grown up in New Orleans. But she was aware of where Highland Village was located, and went to apply for a bartending job.

She walked into BRAVO! just in time to watch the Italian oven being driven to its permanent home in the kitchen.

"I remember it being empty, but there was a card table and a couple of folding chairs," Lesley says. "Honestly, I was going to go work there because Dave asked me to. Because he was my friend and he was going to be the bar manager and it was going to be cool."

She met with David, Dan and Jeff and at the end of the interview Jeff shook her hand.

"Jeff Good was very sincere and he was like 'Thank you, welcome aboard. We're real excited.'"

* * *

While all of the construction was taking place, Dan went back to the menu. Initially, he wanted to have a short menu full of items under $10. But the more shares they sold, the more Jeff pressured him to add expensive items.

"Some of these investors he'd gotten were moneyed people," Dan recalls. "They wanted to come in and spend money and they wanted fish. They wanted steaks. I figured that out, and started adding stuff and raising the prices, and the menu just created itself. There was a demand for it, so we changed to meet the demand."

Part of the challenge was to create different menu items, without having to order specialty ingredients that would only be used in one dish, and possibly go bad before they were used. A good chef takes a larder of product and crosses everything over so it doesn't look the same, but there's less waste.

"You're using a lot of the same product to make different dishes, and I don't think it's obvious. When I look back sometimes on my older menus, it's obvious and I don't like it, but I've loosened up since then," Dan shares.

Dan also had another menu decision that would set the course for BRAVO!

"I had to choose whether I'd do my own baked goods, my own breads, or do my pasta. I couldn't do both because of the time and labor."

Dan chose to make fresh bread every morning at BRAVO!, and offer diners a basket of fresh bread with unlimited refills. The bread he would bake would require a "starter" – fermenters that get the dough to rise. He reached out to a friend in San Francisco, and made a special order for opening week: the fermenters he would use to start his focaccia and baguettes.

"Times are changing, you know, letting people fill up on bread. Probably not the smartest thing as a restaurateur. A lot of people charge for bread. A lot of people don't give you bread. We think completely differently," Dan says.

* * *

Each of the guys had their own area that they were in charge of. Dan was the back of the house manager, in charge of the kitchen and everyone in it, along with ordering ingredients for the food. Jeff was the front of the house manager, in charge of wait staff, and ordering anything for the dining room – like napkins or paper goods. David would be the bar manager, in charge of the bartenders and working with the ABC for their liquor and wine needs.

In Mississippi, the Alcoholic Beverage Control (ABC) is part of the Department of Revenue. It controls what wine and liquor are brought into the state for resale. That means if you want to buy a particular wine for your restaurant, you see if it's being offered through the ABC for purchase, and then you buy it through them.

When David was putting together the wine program at BRAVO! there was only one sheet of wines available for purchase.

"I went to the ABC and said: 'we want better wine. We want to get this special order and really push them,'" David remembers. "We helped push the ABC to start bringing in more product. We convinced them that it would be worth their time and effort to bring these products in."

David was looking to push the boundaries in Jackson when it came to wine; he was a self-admitted "snob" deciding what they would serve at BRAVO! And he held a hard line on what they wouldn't serve, too. On that list? Mussolini Wines (the name has been changed). They were on 90 percent of the restaurant menus in town, and when BRAVO! didn't want to sell their products, the sales representative couldn't understand it.

Mussolini Wine used to be like jug wine, David says today: "They started producing single vineyard wines and that's the thing these guys were trying to push hard. To be honest, I have no doubt those wines were really high quality, because the company has very deep pockets. And they had the ability to buy single vineyard grapes and produce high-quality wines. Looking back on it, I was probably just a wine snob. I don't care what the quality is of the wine. It's Mussolini Wine, and I just will not put that on my menu."

The sales rep would stop by BRAVO! regularly, trying to change David's mind. He would offer David a case of wine, for free, just to try it. David said no.

"They were so persistent, because they knew they would have a venue for their products. But I would not give in. I did not want that product," David says.

THE BRAVO! WAY

One day before the BRAVO! grand opening, David was behind the bar cleaning up. Jeff and Dan were working in the front house and kitchen, when a group of people walked up and knocked on the front door. Jeff looked over at David as he ducks behind the bar.

"Can I help you?" Jeff asked as he opens the door.

The entire group pushed past Jeff and walks into the lounge.

"Hey, this is So and So from New Jersey, and she's the District Muckety Muck and they just wanted to meet you," the Mussolini Wine rep said to Jeff. "Is David here?"

"David's not here right now," Jeff replied.

"We need to talk about your partner, because obviously there's a problem here," So and So from New Jersey said, as he leaned in closer to Jeff. "He doesn't seem to understand. Your partner doesn't seem to understand, you can't have a menu without having Mussolini Wine."

This caused Jeff's blood pressure to start rising. He was already wound tight with all of the stress of building out the restaurant. And while he may be easygoing most of the time, when someone seemingly threatens him or his business, he loses it.

Jeff went completely nuts and started cussing out the entire Mussolini Wine contingent, as he pushed them out the door. When the last person went through the glass door, Jeff yelled: "And don't come back!"

He locked the door, and walked away.

"Man, thanks!" David said as he came out from behind the bar.

They all looked back through the windows to see So and So from New Jersey pacing back and forth on the walkway, talking to the rest of the group. After several minutes, they finally left.

David didn't back down. During his time as Bar Manager, BRAVO! never offered a single Mussolini Wine on its list.

THE BRAVO! WAY

* * *

April 3, 1994
Dear Friends:

    A THOUSAND PARDONS FOR A MOST UNFORTUNATE EVENT!
    Last week, we sent out the invitations for the BRAVO! Grand Opening Party to be held Thursday, April 7. These beautiful invitations were oversized post cards with decorative hand-stamped food and wine images adorning each side. According to the weekend telephone reports, some of you had not received your invitation. A little research found that others had received someone else's invitation stuck to the back of their own invitation. Apparently, the inks were not completely dry on the post cards, and therefore many of the cards adhered to one another when bundled for the post office mailbox.
    WE ARE VERY SORRY IF YOU ARE ONE OF THE PEOPLE THIS AFFECTED. Rest assured, you have been on our guest list from day one, and we very much expect to see you at the party. To this end, please come help us celebrate:
    Thursday, April 7, 1994 from 7:00 p.m. to 10:30 p.m.
    Again, we are very sorry if this has inconvenienced you.
    Ciao!
    Dan, David and Jeff
    P.S. When you come Thursday night, we will show you the invitation. While it may not mail well, it looks great!

[Letter sent to the invited guests for the grand opening.]

* * *

The final days of construction and setup of BRAVO! were a frenzy as the guys worked around the clock to get things ready, especially Jeff who was often found with his punch list.

"I remember quite a few nights of being there all night. I remember being there when the sun came up," Jeff says.

"I basically didn't see Jeff," Debbie adds. "At that point in my marriage, I'd been accustomed to the first year or two that we were married Jeff being out of town so much and then just being home for a little while, and I was working."

Dan was pushing Jeff to get certain elements in place before opening, like training handouts and employment folders. He knew from experience, there would be no moments to do it after BRAVO! opened.

"If you don't get all this stuff done before you open, when you open you're not going to have time," Dan said. "You're going to be in the process of running your restaurant. You're going to be looking at problems that don't have anything to do with finishing the restaurant punch list."

"Dan would say I'm never going to have another moment. That's something that still resonates with me now," Jeff says. "Managers, during your shift if you're working in a restaurant, there's no office time. You're in the restaurant. You should be in the flow all the time. You shouldn't be in back."

"I knew what it took to run a restaurant, and you have to be focused and proactive," Dan said. "You're going to tweak the systems that you put in place before opening, but you better have something in place. Otherwise it will slow you down."

They were going to save money by printing their own menus in house, but Jeff wanted to give them some pizazz.

"We came up with the idea of doing hand-stamped menus," Jeff explains.

A graphic artist created special rubber stamps shaped like food. Team BRAVO! would then use artist's ink and stamp the outer craft paper folders that would contain the menu.

"We had two different nights of painting parties. We would open up some wine and we'd lay out the things and we'd stamp them and wait for them to dry. The idea was we leave it overnight and that would be dry in the morning," Jeff remembers.

But the artist's ink never completely dried, no matter how long they left it alone. When you set the menus on tables without tablecloths, which also had water glasses that sweat, and olive oil that gets everywhere, the craft paper would quickly become a runny mess. So they tried lamination.

As they were getting the menus ready, the Tuscan-inspired mural was being finished in the lounge area. Mississippi artist Lynn Green Root created a 30-foot long brightly colored, abstract mural that took up both walls in the lounge, floor to ceiling. It highlights the terra cotta roof tiles on Tuscan villas. There are rolling hillsides with vineyards and flowers, all under the Tuscan sun. It was a stunning addition to the restaurant.

Directly opposite the mural, on the other side of the restaurant, was the wood-fired oven that came from Italy. The surrounding wall had been painted to look like a terra cotta finish. To further enhance the "open kitchen" concept, a counter was installed right in front of the oven. You could sit and have your meal, along with a front-row view of what went on in the kitchen. There were no side "walls" in the dining room. Those had been knocked out and were replaced with windows. Huge floor to ceiling windows on both sides, and in the afternoon, you got a great view of the sunset over Interstate 55 to the west.

Dan's friend from San Francisco flew in the week before they opened, toting a cooler full of the bread fermenters. He would help get the breads started and stick around through opening day.

It was all coming together nicely, but the day before the grand opening, there was something very important missing from the dining room: the booths and banquettes that made up nearly half of the seating. They hadn't arrived yet.

Jeff got on the phone with the furniture rep and asked where his dining room was. "We're opening tomorrow and we have no booths or banquettes!" Jeff told the guy. "You've known about this forever! You need to get these things in here!"

Amazingly, they did show up, later that day.

"Somehow it's miraculous. When people open restaurants, somehow it always comes together," Jeff says. "I don't understand why it can't be done two days earlier, but it has to be done on Wednesday!"

Everything was now in place for the grand opening of BRAVO! Italian Restaurant and Bar. But opening day would be anything but smooth.

Photo © Tom and Kasi Beck, all rights reserved

BRAVO! Warm Tomato Bruschetta

For the crostini
1 loaf crusty bread such as a baguette or ciabatta, thinly sliced (2-3 slices per person)
¼ cup extra virgin olive oil
1 clove garlic, peeled and crushed
For the topping
2 large ripe tomatoes, large dice
½ small red onion, sliced
2 cloves garlic, peeled and thinly sliced
1 tablespoon basil leaves, julienned
1 teaspoon chili pepper flakes
2 tablespoons extra virgin olive oil
Salt and ground black pepper to taste
2 teaspoons aged balsamic vinegar
1 tablespoon water
1 tablespoon cold, unsalted butter
Freshly grated Parmesan cheese to finish

THE BRAVO! WAY

For the crostini, use a pastry brush to lightly brush the oil onto both sides of the bread slices. With your hand, rub the clove of raw garlic on the slices to impart the garlic essence to the bread.

On a hot grill, "mark" the bread on both sides until it is toasted and crunchy and has grill marks, but is not burned. If you do not have easy access to a grill, bake the bread in a 350-degree oven on a cookie sheet until golden brown. Be sure to turn the bread over and toast both sides.

For the topping, heat a sauté skillet over medium-high heat. Add the olive oil and bring to smoking. Add the tomatoes, onion, garlic, salt and pepper and chili flakes. Stir occasionally, using a wooden spoon to mash the tomatoes some to release their liquid.

Add the balsamic vinegar and water and continue to cook until the tomatoes break down some. Finish by swirling in the cold butter, which will thicken the liquid in your pan. Pour the hot tomato mixture over your crostini.

Grate fresh Parmesan over the top and enjoy!

Serves 4

Note from Chef Dan Blumenthal: *If I had a dollar for every time Debbie Good ordered this appetizer over the years! Another true BRAVO! classic, this is just plain, good Italian comfort food.*

Opening day at BRAVO! Photo courtesy Jeff Good
Front row (L-R) David Blumenthal, Jeff Good, Dan Blumenthal

CHAPTER 3

CHE è PER PRANZO?

> **BRAVO! will serve creative, delicious, high-quality food in Jackson's most visually stimulating atmosphere. The goal is to make the BRAVO! experience truly exceptional from start to finish. All BRAVO! employees shall know that passion (the desire to be the best), perfection (the training to be the best) and performance (the execution of that perfection) are the three legs of the stool on which Bravo's reputation will stand.**
> **[From the BRAVO! business plan]**

Dan, Jeff and David had worked tirelessly on getting the physical restaurant ready for opening day—construction on the space, setting up the kitchen equipment and tables. But there were other, softer setups that needed to be put in place; like the wait stations. They also needed to train the team on the BRAVO! concept.

"We split the baby – front house, back house," Jeff says. "Brian Heffner and William Bennett helped me immensely with the front house because I'm doing punch lists on construction and I don't know what I'm doing."

Brian had worked with David at 400 East Capitol. He and William set up stations for the wait staff, because they had experience in that area.

Back in the kitchen, Dan had been working with some employees for three months – training them on cooking a style of food that they weren't used to. Dan was teaching the kitchen and wait staff about risotto and polenta. He showed them what a Portobello mushroom was.

"And focaccia bread. People hadn't seen that before. It was about introducing a staff to something that they had never seen before," Jeff adds. "The training was very kitchen-focused because we were really about food. We made that clear that this restaurant was going to be about food."

The BRAVO! business plan laid out the front of the house training: "Bravo! will be a full-service restaurant. Customers will be greeted at the door by a hostess specifically instructed to make each guest feel welcome and special. Whenever possible, patrons will be greeted by name and/or personal acknowledgement.

"When there is a waiting list for tables, the hostess will take the guest's name and show them to the bar/cocktail area. Upon returning to the hostess stand, the hostess shall make some form of personal note next to the guest's name. This will allow the hostess to specifically pick the guest and his/her party out of the crowd. The guest is tapped on the shoulder and informed his/her personal table is ready. This personal touch eliminates tacky intercom systems. This small indulgence sets a special tone, and reaffirms our quality focus."

Pesto is now a staple on the BRAVO! menu, but in the beginning – Dan needed to hold a class on it. Jeff walked into the kitchen as Dan patiently showed his team how to handle basil and explained just how expensive pine nuts were, meaning: don't waste them. Jeff watched in awe until he couldn't stand it anymore and shouted: "This is the greatest thing I've ever seen! We're making food!"

"I was just so excited," Jeff says. "A lot of restaurants don't deal with a lot of raw product and herbs and lettuces that were different."

Dan made everything on the menu from scratch, including the salad dressings, and would then put dishes up on the counter for the wait staff to try. He was more than ready to get the restaurant open and start feeding paying customers.

"I'd never opened a restaurant before, but I knew what I was doing. I felt confident doing it," Dan says. "At that point, I thought we could pull it off. I don't recall being nervous."

He did get extremely aggravated with Jeff on opening day, however.

Thursday, April 7, 1994 was a beautiful spring day in Jackson, Mississippi. It's one of the two times of the year when the weather is downright perfect. That day, the skies were clear. The temperatures were in the 60s and there was practically no humidity.

BRAVO! was buzzing as everyone set up for their first group of guests coming at seven o'clock. Jeff was in frenzy mode, because he wanted to make sure this moment was preserved for the future. He was running around, insisting that the entire staff go outside into the parking lot and stand beneath the BRAVO! sign for a "class picture". It's the one thing Dan remembers from opening day.

"More than anything getting that picture done, because everything had to be stopped. Interrupted. Everyone had to be brought outside around five o'clock," Dan says.

"We were all under a lot of stress and strain," David remembers about opening day. "I look at that picture and see how tired I was. And I just remember being so exhausted. I was delirious."

Opening day was also a blur for Debbie Good. She was about to start her new second job as an unpaid hostess for the restaurant and had raced home from teaching school to change, before heading to BRAVO!.

"I remember pulling up right before they did their lineup," Debbie says. "I was in the parking lot and Jeff had everybody out there for the big picture with everybody dressed up. And it was Jeff, Dan and Dave standing there with all the people."

Not long after the picture was taken, they opened the doors for their first customers.

The buzz about BRAVO! had been spreading for weeks, thanks to word of mouth and a media blitz by Jeff.

"There were huge waits," Debbie recalls about the first week. "People would hand me a 20 dollar bill, or more sometimes, to get a table. Every once in a while I would take it and I would give it to the girl who worked with me."

Behind the bar, Lesley Tolar and the bartending team were getting slammed.

"I was there opening night and it was a shit show," she says. "We didn't know what we were doing. There was a new point of sale system that none of us really knew how to work. And I had not eaten any of the food. I didn't know how to ring anything up, but we just sort of figured it out. We all figured it out."

The guests were unaware of the struggles on opening night, especially two of the restaurant's biggest fans: Janice and Buddy Blumenthal.

"It was very exciting," Buddy recalls. "It's like a big cocktail party. I'd imagine the majority of people in the room or at least a quarter of the people in the room had money in it. It was full of energy! And the staff was up for it, and the kitchen – it was like a big party."

To get people in the door for the opening, the guys offered the food at cost – much cheaper prices than on the formal menu. And the place filled up quickly.

"People waited in line in the bar area," Janice says.

"They were waiting out on the patio balcony just to get in," Buddy adds.

"It was totally new and novel and then you know, word of mouth," Janice says.

Buddy says he knew the place would be successful the first time he had a meal there.

"From the very beginning, all you had to do was sit down and have a meal and enjoy the quality of the food and see people around you, and you know whether something's going to go or not," Buddy says.

BRAVO! was different from other restaurants in the area. If you stood in the lounge area, you could see all the way back to the open kitchen. There were no side rooms, curtains or cubbyholes where customers were squirreled away for dinner. There was scored concrete on the floor and there were no tablecloths on the tables, so you could see the tabletops. The dining room was non-smoking, but you could still smoke in the lounge.

"We got a lot of pushback from people on that, because they had never heard of a restaurant that didn't have a smoking section," Jeff says.

There was also no dress code. You would get the same service no matter if you showed up in jeans or a tuxedo.

"There were a lot of pokes to what the market was used to. Also we were completely unknown," Jeff adds.

On each table there would be a bottle of rosemary-infused olive oil, something that BRAVO! would eventually sell to the public. When the waiter or waitress came to your table to introduce themselves, they would fill your water glass and drop off a basket of hot, fresh bread: focaccia and baguette slices, regardless of what you would go on to order. They would then answer any questions about the menu, and there were many questions.

The menu was large, and contained a glossary titled: Che è per Pranzo? (What's for Dinner?) It described balsamic vinegar, biscotti, focaccia bread, Fontina cheese, gnocchi, mascarpone cheese, pancetta, polenta, prosciutto and risotto. The drink menu was almost as big as the dinner menu with beers, specialty cocktails, Torani-flavored Italian sodas, coffee drinks and a wine list that contained value wines not found on any other list in town. David had also set up several wines by the glass that included red and white, sparkling, dessert wines, ports and cognacs.

Service was also different at BRAVO! Customers weren't put on the spot to pick a dinner entrée right away. The wait staff would focus on the appetizers and drinks, giving the diner a chance to try something new. While the appetizer is put into the ordering system, you then have more time to go over the menu.

Jeff had harkened back to his time at The Other Place and The Lighthouse, and trained every one of his waiters and waitresses how to sell the entrees, by describing them in great detail. The wait staff could suggest popular items, specials or personal favorites. He was also out on the floor, waiting tables and talking to customers every day.

In the kitchen, Dan had trained his team how to make every single dish on the menu from scratch, and get it out to the table in 18 minutes or less. The BRAVO! standard. He was hands-on from the very beginning as the head chef.

The first three to four months, Jeff was getting real-time negative feedback on the food, and anxiety would kick in.

"The folks who weren't buying into what we were doing were very vocal," Jeff says.

Ever the salesman, Jeff would run back to the kitchen when he'd get negative feedback.

"Dan, they can't stand this dish, they say they don't understand what we're doing here, you need to change this," Jeff would tell Dan in a panic.

"Jeff, you gotta' have faith in what we're doing here," Dan would say calmly. "We decided to do this, I know what I'm doing. We gotta' stay the course, trust me."

"I didn't have my ears open. I wasn't listening to them, partly my young arrogance, but it may have been why we succeeded," Dan says now. "I had done this food and done it well in a huge market. I knew if I stayed the course, somebody would get it."

Jeff trusted Dan, but he would also send the occasional "special request" into the kitchen from a customer. Dan's blood pressure would shoot up.

"I came from a very chef-driven environment where you ate what the chef cooked. You didn't tell the chef what to cook. You just didn't do that," Dan says.

Jeff wanted Dan to cook whatever the customer requested, and in the early days Dan would refuse.

"If you want me to cook shit and put it on a plate, I'll do it. But I'm not going to stand behind it," Dan would tell Jeff.

Jeff would tell Dan to do it anyway, because the customer was willing to pay for it. He would eventually wear Dan down on the matter. Most of the time, the customer was happy. But on those other occasions they weren't, Dan would also be unhappy: "What upsets me the most is when somebody changes something radically and then doesn't like it."

There are customers who have ordered things that weren't even on the menu. Things that Dan wasn't too keen on cooking, but he would eventually get with the program and make what they requested.

"They eat it and like it, and they come back," Dan says.

As for official restaurant critics, there weren't too many in Jackson.

"If we were in a bigger city, they probably would have beaten us up. There are twenty different critics in a big city writing for twenty different rags. But it's Jackson. You've got a couple of free press type deals and you got *The Clarion-Ledger*, which had the one food critic in town – 'Epicurious.' If you nailed 'Epicurious' you were fine," Dan explains.

"Epicurious" was among the first diners in the door when they opened BRAVO! to the general public on April 12, 1994. The restaurant critic would go on to give BRAVO! four out of five stars.

"We were bringing something to town that was new and different and maybe didn't suit him 100 percent but it was generally succeeding," Dan says.

People would pack the restaurant every night for the next few weeks, testing the limits of the staff in the kitchen, and in the front of the house. If a customer asked about the fancy wood-fired oven, they weren't just told about it, they were taken back to the kitchen area to look at it up close, and even meet Chef Dan.

The three partners were each working in their areas, from open to close, every day. Dan was in the kitchen, cooking. Jeff was on the dining room floor, waiting tables. David was in the bar, making drinks and pouring wine.

"They worked all the time," Linda Kay Russell says. "There were no managers, it was David, Dan and Jeff."

"My biggest complaint was that the money was all messed up. I like my bills all lined up in the same direction," she laughs.

When Linda Kay arrived at eight in the morning, she would take the money from the night before and put together the bank deposit and figure up the entries for the general ledger. Everything she did was done by hand.

Linda Kay was also a stickler for her way of doing things.

"Jeff would laugh at me because I want the ones a certain way – 25 ones put together. I was going to re-count them anyway, because I'm quite controlling."

Linda Kay was working part-time, so when the guys would get there at 10 a.m., she was waiting for them with her questions before she left for the day.

"I was always behind. I think I would get three hours out of the day, but it didn't matter, because the three guys were there, on top of things," Linda Kay says. "They knew what was going on in the restaurant. It wasn't like we had to worry about fraud or theft. We were making money. Dan knew it. Dan could tell you the sales every day. He's really on top of the numbers."

The three men worked every day in the restaurant, waiting for people to catch on to what they were doing. That happened around month six or seven.

"People started saying 'This is amazing!' That's the point where we caught the early adopters, the mainstream was starting to understand what we were doing and the word of mouth was getting out," Jeff says.

They were also perfecting the process. In the first few months, things weren't always executing well, but they worked out the bugs and it was becoming a well-oiled machine, at least as far as the diners noticed.

* * *

It's Here!
This is it.
The menu.
The best of traditional and innovative Italian fare.
The wines.
A definite departure.
Join us for lunch and dinner, or drop in for a cappuccino after some serious shopping.
A resounding BRAVO!
BRAVO! Italian Restaurant and Bar is now open on the upper level of the Plaza of Highland Village.
[Advertisement announcing BRAVO! was open]

* * *

Several months after opening, the guys decided working seven days a week was going to kill them. So, they would each take turns taking time off. David would fill in for Dan at the chef's position, or manage the front of the house for Jeff. Jeff would manage the bar, and on Wednesdays, he would expedite in the kitchen for Dan. They also needed a break from each other, because they were getting on each other's last nerve.

One Wednesday, Jeff was hung over from the night before, and by 11:30 a.m., the kitchen was already slammed or "in the weeds." Jeff is scrambling to move the food out to the dining room when Dan comes in. It's his day off, so he's wearing shorts and a t-shirt, looking totally relaxed.

"He starts critiquing everything I'm doing and then he really starts to lay in on me and just stands there, not doing a thing. Not helping. He's just there to harass me," Jeff remembers.

Jeff gets so frustrated with him, he drops the towel he was holding, cussed at Dan, walked out of the restaurant and went home. Jeff says it's the maddest he's ever been at his partner.

Dan doesn't remember that exact incident but admits he was "probably pushing his buttons," something he does on a regular basis.

"The stress you're under, and me coming in that time of day," Dan says.

"That's the thing about my ego is: I'll work harder than anyone, but if you push me, I'm just going to act out like a kid. Be childish about it," Jeff admits. "Just talking smack. It's just fun, but when you add in the stress about the business. Because it is a partnership, it's hard."

Jeff was also trying to out-work everybody else in the restaurant, especially David.

"I could just work harder and longer than anybody. I'd sacrifice more. I wouldn't take shortcuts. We're going to do things the right way," Jeff says.

He admits he would get passive-aggressive about it with David, simply by offering to lock up every night.

"Okay, I'll go if you've got it," David would say, oblivious that anything was wrong. He would have stayed to lock up, but Jeff offered, so David would leave.

And that just aggravated Jeff even more.

"I didn't know how to deal with the issues that one of the 33.33 percent partners didn't have the same fire in his belly for the daily grind that the other two of us had," Jeff said.

Looking back on it now, Jeff admits the passive-aggressiveness was silly because he could have gone home at 10 o'clock, instead of midnight. But Jeff says he had something to prove to himself.

"There are very few people who are wired with the masochism that's required to put this together. It's a non-stop grind," Jeff shares.

David was stuck in the bar every single day and was feeling the pull of that daily grind.

"One thing about the restaurant business is the repetitive nature of it. You do the same thing every single day. You make a huge mess. At the end of the day you clean it all up, turn the lights off and lock the doors and come back the next day and do the exact same thing," he says.

If you're not prepared for that, then it's hard: "You've got to be able to deal with the grind. A lot of people just can't deal with it."

"When you're 30 years old, you think the world revolves around you," David adds. "At times I wish I hadn't been obstinate or stubborn about certain things. I think I could have been more flexible. There were times I worked really hard, but then there were times when I probably didn't work hard enough. I think anybody who has ever worked with Dan and Jeff would agree – it's really hard to work that hard."

Dan was prepared for the daily grind, and made a decision when he moved back to town that would ultimately help him in the first two years of opening BRAVO! He had moved back in with his parents, about a mile away from the restaurant. He knew opening the restaurant was going to be intense and since he only made $25,000 that first year, it was convenient living just a mile away, and it would save him money.

"All I did was work and go home. It was never the plan to stay. It was just like: I'm going to be working my ass off and not have a life, I might as well drive home and crash," Dan shares.

"We saw little of him at that time," Buddy says. "Our thing is we'd go to BRAVO! practically every Sunday night and that's when we used to see Dan."

Janice would know when he had been home, because of the dirty laundry. She did his laundry in order to keep him away from her machines and to keep him from doing laundry at all hours of the night, waking up the rest of the household. This was different from when he was a teenager, working at Wendy's – when she made him leave his work clothes outside because they smelled like grease and hamburgers. His BRAVO! gear was mostly just sweaty from hard work.

"My world was BRAVO! All I cared about was who came in. I'm just looking at the number of people coming and going and making sure the food goes out the way I want it and it's timed right and that the service is good," Dan says.

It also helps that Dan is the "numbers guy" in the partnership.

"If I asked Dan how many of something he served yesterday, he knows," Buddy says. "He's keeping score."

* * *

July 14, 1994
Dear BRAVO! Limited Partner:

    As we proposed to you when soliciting your support, it has been our intent to open a top quality restaurant in Jackson, serving creative and exceptional food, with a "best of class" staff, in a striking physical environment. It has also been our intent to achieve this status while earning an above average profit. Since our opening to the general public April 12, 1994, Dan, David and I are very pleased with the progress we have made toward these goals and it is with great excitement that we share the results of our efforts.

    Our final construction figures ran 10% over budget, thus eroding our working capital account prior to opening. However, our phenomenal financial performance immediately replenished this account, and we are on our way to a truly outstanding first year, as long as we can maintain and grow our sales while continuing to manage our costs.

    Overall, business is well above our expectations. We are consistently busy and continue to receive high accolades from our customers. We have been receiving direct customer feedback through the use of comment cards presented to each table with the check. I have enclosed copies of a few of the returned comment cards for your reference.

    As we move through the summer and into the fall, our objective will be to grow our market presence beyond the borders of the Northeast Jackson sector. We will achieve this through selective advertising and through continued community involvement and goodwill.

    Please continue to support us by joining us for lunch and dinner, telling your friends and co-workers about us, purchasing gift certificates to give as gifts or work-related bonuses and talking us up in the community at large. Dan, David and I are committed to making BRAVO! the most successful restaurant in Mississippi, a status we cannot achieve without your help!

    Respectfully yours,
    Jeff Good

* * *

Dan and Jeff were only thirty years old when BRAVO! opened. David was twenty-seven and most of the employees were around the same age as they were.

Lesley Tolar celebrated her 25th birthday the week after BRAVO! opened.

"I was just a kid," she says. "It was always cool for me to be around somebody like Jeff because he was like one of us."

"Those were fun times and it was an amazing experience opening that restaurant. We're all pretty much the same age as a lot of the employees were. So we're leading people our own age," Jeff says.

He was also very particular about how expected things to be run in the dining room, an attitude matched by Dan in the back of the house.

"Jeff has always known exactly what he wants and how he expects things to be," Lesley says.

When someone went rogue on waiting tables or presentation of food, Jeff would walk up to them and say: "What you're doing is not BRAVO!" or "That's not BRAVO!"

When a bartender, who had been reading a "get rich quick" book, suggested they make changes to everything in the restaurant; Jeff turned to him and said calmly: "Do not fuck with my concept."

Where Dan and Jeff were always going at top speed, David would take his time, and was much more laid back. It earned him the nickname "Dr. Slow" from his brother Dan.

Dan would also get onto David for his morning ritual of coffee and reading the newspaper. That would have been fine at home, but David was doing it in the office.

"He'd be back in the office at eight o'clock having a coffee and reading the newspaper, and employees would go back there, sit down and grab parts of the paper and start reading it with him," Dan explains.

Dan would tell David that this wasn't a good idea, that they were paying people to work and they needed to come in and get to work, not sit around for an hour or two.

"You're asking people to clock in and immediately start working hard, and you're back there reading a newspaper and having coffee," Dan would tell his brother. "You can't set this example."

David didn't want to rock the boat, so Dan would have to go in and flush people out of the office, telling them to get to work.

David also avoided confrontation in the bar. He had worked with Lesley and Phil Petrignani at 400 East Capitol, and hired them as two of the original bartenders at BRAVO! There was a third bartender at the beginning that Lesley and Phil didn't know very well, and they didn't hang out with him after work – so they decided to vote him out of the bar.

"We told Dave we didn't want him in the bar anymore, and Dave just moved him out to the floor," Lesley says. "We chose who we wanted. We said we want Scott Barranti to come back here."

Lesley says she and Phil ran all over David, not to be mean, but because they wanted to work with whom they wanted to work with. And David never told them no.

"Jeff on the other hand, in the early days, was much more hotheaded than he is now. He would have epic fits," Lesley remembers.

One of those epic fits centered on a radio in the kitchen. Dan's rule was: no radios in the kitchen, but there was a boombox that the dishwashers and prep guys would listen to all the time. When it got too loud, Jeff would go back to the kitchen and say: "How many times have I told you to turn this down?" He would then turn down the radio and go back to work.

One day, Jeff was standing at the tables in the dining room closest to the kitchen. He could hear the music coming from the back, and he became livid. He marched back into the kitchen, unplugged the radio, took it out back and grabbed a ladder leaning against the building.

"There's to be NO FUCKING RADIOS!" Jeff yelled as he smashed the radio to bits with the ladder.

He immediately felt remorse, and started pacing around the kitchen, talking a mile a minute.

"I'm sorry I broke your radio and I will replace it, but you cannot bring it back up here," Jeff said to the dishwasher, as he paced.

The employees were all just standing around looking at each other until one of the guys said: "Hey man, I think that's your radio. That's not my radio."

Turns out, it was the radio Jeff had brought up to the building during the time of construction, and had forgotten all about it.

* * *

Countless hours of planning, fundraising and backbreaking manual labor went into the creation of BRAVO!. The vision Jeff, David and I had was a contemporary, cosmopolitan restaurant offering a casual, warm and inviting atmosphere.

So far, BRAVO! has enjoyed tremendous success. My only regret is that we have not yet established as broad an appeal as we had originally hoped. We work constantly to fine-tune our operation, so that no one need feel intimidated by our cuisine. We want everyone to feel as though they can come to BRAVO!, spend a little or a lot, and find a dish or dishes, which will bring them back time and time again.

With this in mind, my pledge to you is this: without compromise, I am committed to bringing you the freshest, most innovative, visually stimulating cuisine in Jackson. My goal is not to confuse or intimidate, but to challenge your palates with existing combinations of flavors. I have always believed that part of the whole aura of dining out rests in the enjoyment of adventurous cuisine, which is not practical or simple to cook at home.

Over time, every restaurant takes on its own, distinct personality. Although BRAVO! is still an infant, it no doubt evokes a distinct vision in the minds of its clientele. In keeping with this, it is not our intention to directly compete with other Jackson restaurants specializing in steaks, seafood, fast food, family-style buffets or blue-plate lunches. We are what we are and we firmly believe in the direction we have chosen.

In closing I want to personally thank you for your support thus far, and look forward to serving you well into the future.

Mangia Bene!
Dan
["A six month retrospective from Chef Dan" in the Fall/Winter 1994 newsletter The BRAVO! Buzz]

* * *

BRAVO! wasn't just getting buzz as the hot new restaurant in town, its bar was the hot new nightclub. The cool lounge combined with the happy hour pricing that David put together and people would be five deep at the bar on most nights.

"There were a couple of times in that first couple of years you could not get into that restaurant, because of the mob at the bar," Buddy Blumenthal recalls.

"That place was packed every night. At four o'clock in the afternoon, people started trickling in. If something was going on outside that bar, we didn't know anything about it. Because we weren't moving from that bar until we were closed. We didn't eat. We didn't have a sip of water or go to the bathroom," Lesley says.

Jeff was married and David had just gotten engaged, but Dan was single, good-looking and part owner of the hottest new restaurant in town. He was a draw for all the single ladies. There would be times when he would close the kitchen, but the bar was still slammed with customers.

"Dan was young and he had all kinds of girls who would come to the bar," Lesley remembers. "He would come into the bar and stand right in front of the main service well, where we made the drinks. He would stand there with his arms crossed, and start looking at the crowd and saying 'Hey ladies, you having a good time? Everybody enjoying themselves?'"

Lesley would get aggravated with him because he'd just stand there, in the middle of her service area, and not move.

"Dan you have to move! Go over there and talk to them, just get out!" Lesley would tell him. She says she was half-tempted to stand in his expo station the next day and block his work.

Other times Dan and Jeff would stay after closing to hang out with the employees.

"We were wild people back then. I mean we hardly ever slept," Lesley remembers. "We made 500 dollars at the bar and by the next morning we each only had 75! We were going gambling. Dan never went, but Jeff was always the ringleader. At least once a week a pack of people from BRAVO! went to Vicksburg to the boats after we closed. We would stay until the sun came up."

The staff would also hang out together on their day off, which was Monday.

"We had this tradition on Mondays. Everybody would sleep really late because we probably stayed up all night then we would get together and have lunch," Lesley recalls.

Around four o'clock in the afternoon, everyone would end up in a co-worker's studio apartment on Manship Street. There was only a bed and a recliner in this tiny apartment, but every Monday it would be crammed full of people who worked at BRAVO! and some of their friends.

"There'd be loads of people. People sitting on the floor, all over the bed, and we drank vodka all day," Lesley says. "Somebody would show up with vodka and we would just shake it up with lemons and put in a martini glass. We were basically just drinking straight vodka all day."

Eventually someone would decide they were hungry, and the whole crew would go to the Cherokee Drive Inn on State Street.

"We would drink beers and eat hotdogs and hamburgers and play pool and then go home and pass out," Lesley adds. "We were the classic restaurant people, if we weren't at work. We were really good at our jobs. We were spot on when we were in there waiting on people and then when we clocked out, we were cussing and drinking."

Some of the employees started the Superband Wasteband with David Blumenthal on guitar. The band wrote their own songs and would play gigs around Jackson. They even had their own backup dancers, which included Lesley and her friend Tara.

* * *

Things with Jeff and Debbie had become strained, because he spent all of his time at the restaurant. They were also bringing home next to nothing, because those first two years, he barely took a paycheck. And she made no money in her second job as hostess for BRAVO!

"They paid one hostess, and I was there six, sometimes seven nights a week. I'd be there after I finished school. I'd go home to freshen up, then run to Highland Village and do whatever I had to do there," Debbie says.

But when she was done with her hostess shift, she had to go home and get some sleep before school the next day. Jeff would often stay late at work.

"I almost got divorced because I lost myself in something that gave me incredible instantaneous satisfaction," Jeff admits. "Complete control. A challenge. A goal."

That challenge? BRAVO! The restaurant itself.

Debbie started referring to the restaurant as the "other woman" or "Bravette."

"We're making goal on a regular basis and that positive feedback was the complete explosion of ego and competition. And a group of people looked up to me. My own family," Jeff says.

Debbie and Jeff had been trying to start their own family. Even though they were fighting about how much time he spent at the restaurant, she had been taking a series of hormone treatments and pills. Nothing had worked.

"There was a particular enzyme they were trying to track and it was negative, it just didn't register," Jeff explains. "And every time she had blood work they said 'We've taken you all the way up, there's nothing more we can do.'"

Debbie went to see her doctor for a checkup and blood test. Her doctor was going to refer her to a specialist. She and Jeff both knew that would mean expensive in vitro fertilization treatments that may or may not work.

The next morning the doctor called her and said: "You need to come back in here."

"There's something really weird with your blood, and I don't want to scare you but we need to do another test because all of a sudden the enzyme we're trying to track, it just all of a sudden appeared and is way up," the doctor continued.

It turns out the reason it was "weird" was because Debbie was pregnant.

A Wednesday morning, not long after they found out she was pregnant, Jeff and Debbie went to the doctor for an internal ultrasound, to make sure everything was okay. Jeff was wearing his chef outfit because he had to go expedite the food at BRAVO! later. He was standing in the doorway as the nurse began the scan.

"Okay, well there's one," the nurse said and continued scanning.

"Okay, there's the other," she smiled.

"The other what?" Jeff asked as sweat broke out on his forehead.

"Now is that a third..." the nurse started to say, and Jeff grabbed hold of the doorjamb. "No, no, no. It's just two. You're having twins."

They were shocked. They went from *trying* to have kids to having two at the same time!

Out of an abundance of caution, Jeff told Debbie he no longer wanted her working the hostess stand, since it was right next to the bar, which was a smoking area.

Debbie was happy to no longer work at BRAVO! and was looking forward to getting back to just being a teacher and preparing for her twins.

Jeff says his personal best day in the past 25 years was the day his twin girls were born – Carly and Alex.

"Somebody brought us two wreaths and put them on the outside of the door at BRAVO! Two girl wreaths. The customer base was just as thrilled as I was," Jeff beams. "We were so proud. It was amazing. People knew us, and they cared about us, and they wanted to celebrate us. That's a real important time."

THE BRAVO! WAY

Jeff would also make a major life change within a few months of the girls' births – he would stop drinking altogether.

* * *

Dan is walking through the kitchen, trying to have a conversation with someone, but he keeps getting distracted and his voice trails off, as something catches his eye. He stops to pick up trash from the floor next to the garbage can. He stops to wipe down the prep station. He stops in the walk-in cooler to take produce out of boxes and stock the shelves, then break down the boxes. He wipes down another counter then tells the dishwasher to get a broom and sweep up around his area.

Dan is a clean freak.

"The thing about BRAVO! that's so amazing is the kitchen gets completely broken down and cleaned, every night," Lesley shares. "Every Monday there is a deep clean, in the bar, the restaurant, the kitchen."

Dan designed the kitchen so the floors could be hosed down, scrubbed and squeegeed off – every night. The kitchen staff also moves every piece of equipment out of the hot line area and sweeps and scrubs underneath. Then they wipe down every counter, every hood, and every surface with degreaser. They take a wire brush and degreaser to the grill – every night.

Everything is taken apart on Mondays for the deep clean. In the front of the house: the windows and walls are wiped down and scrubbed; cabinets are emptied out and scrubbed inside and out with degreaser; the air vents and air returns are scrubbed; tables and chairs are scrubbed and fixed – top and bottom; every surface is scrubbed, buffed or degreased.

In the kitchen, they take the hood apart then scrub it with degreaser and pressure wash it. The vents are taken out and cleaned. Everything on shelves inside and outside of the coolers are cleaned and organized. Stovetops and grill grates are cleaned of carbonized debris using degreaser and a pressure washer.

They change the filter on the cooler compressor every week – something Dan says most restaurants don't do. He thinks it's important because you're dealing with perishable food, and the more clean filters, the better.

"That is the cleanest restaurant you'll ever go into," Lesley adds. "There are a lot of restaurants you don't want to go back into the kitchen."

"Dirt is stupid, it always hides in the same spot," Dan tells everyone who works for him. He's even been known to wad up money and throw it behind stations or under tables for employees to find – if they're doing their job and cleaning the right way.

"One thing that bugs me is when servers drop silverware, then don't pick it up off the floor," Dan says.

To prove a point, he'll put a five-dollar bill on the floor near the garbage can and see how long it takes a server to notice. It's often there hours later.

"Servers don't ever look down," he says.

Jon Pixler joined BRAVO! as a sauté cook. He had worked in other restaurants before, but had never seen a cleaning regimen like Dan's. To see just how far Dan would go to have a clean kitchen, the cooks started a bet: what if someone hid a slice of pepperoni behind the wall clock in the kitchen? How long would it take Dan to find it?

Pixler took that bet and would be the one to hide a pepperoni slice behind the clock.

"Dan would just randomly walk up, take the clock down and wipe it all down, and sure enough – there was the pepperoni. He had discovered it within an hour," Lesley laughs.

No one said a word as Dan stood in the kitchen, looking at the pepperoni and trying to determine the trajectory that would have caused a pepperoni slice to fly out of the adjoining room where the food was made, and lodge itself behind the wall clock.

"It's so random, who takes down the wall clock?" Pixler asks.

Pixler would go on to put more pepperoni slices behind the clock several more times, confounding Dan who would find it within an hour every single time.

After closing, Dan would go around to every station and if he found any dirt or "gross stuff" at all, he would sweep it up and put it in your mailbox with a note: "This is what I found last night."

"It is that level of clean," Pixler says. "I learned a lot from Dan. I learned 'cleanliness is next to godliness.'"

Cleanliness is also next to "Danliness." Dan holds a formal inspection of the BRAVO! kitchen every Thursday afternoon, and he doesn't give anyone a pass unless the kitchen is spotless. He has his checklist and goes through every little thing.

"No one does it like we do, in my experience. It's the way I'm programmed. I guess I'm a little anal retentive," Dan smiles.

Even though he was in the kitchen, Jon Pixler also learned a lot from Jeff Good. The first lesson he learned was probably the most memorable.

One night, after he had shut down the sauté stove, customers came in and placed a kitchen order. Pixler was frustrated and walked back to the kitchen, muttering something under his breath that Jeff heard.

Jeff walked up to Pixler, who was thinking: "Just shut up Jon."

But this was a kinder, gentler Jeff. He didn't yell. He didn't lose his cool. He pulled a picture of his twins out of his wallet and showed it to Jon. "Do you see them?" Jeff asked him.

"Yes sir."

"These are my daughters, and this is what's going to put them through college," Jeff told Pixler.

"Yessir, I'm sorry."

That's all Jeff said before walking away. Pixler went back to the sauté stove and turned everything back on to get the order done.

"He knew how to motivate me. That really resonated with me because this dude really cares about his restaurant and more importantly, he's not above and beyond those people walking in the door after we were closed," Pixler says. "Important lesson learned."

THE BRAVO! WAY

"I've learned through experience. I've been through the crucible in every possible way. I've got varicose veins, a herniated disk and almost lost my marriage and alcoholism and everything. Just doing the work and being there every day," Jeff shares. "The culture of 'getting to yes' and 'do the right thing' and telling the truth and 'speaking truth to power' and all of those things I believe, they started to manifest themselves because I was there every day for five years."

Dan, David and Jeff had been working non-stop and Dan was getting a little restless. He started thinking of the original BRAVO! concept that was more like a café. They had been growing talent within the restaurant, and would soon pay off their initial BRAVO! investors. What if they launched another restaurant concept?

"When you have good people that work for you, inevitably the good ones want to move up. So in order to keep them, you have to create jobs for them," Dan says. "That's when you begin to say 'hey, I've got this idea for another restaurant and I have the people to run it.'"

Dan had been the chef at BRAVO! for years, but if he opened another restaurant with his partners, he couldn't be in two places at once. They would have to find a chef to lead the new restaurant.

* * *

August 15, 1997
Dear BRAVO! Limited Partner:
 Enclosed you will find a check which means a great deal to us...
 The cutting of this check signifies that we have fulfilled our promise to pay back 100% of your investment in BRAVO!, in addition to an 8% per year interest payment, and an annual tax rebate at 39.6% of each year's net income. <u>All in all your $10,000 investment has yielded a total of $14,216</u> in just over three years and you will continue to receive payments on 55% of the cash flow as long as the business exists!
 What means so much to us, is that your initial show of faith by investing in three guys with a dream has now come full circle. We have kept our financial commitment to each of you, and by doing so, we are now entitled to participate in the financial

success we have worked to tirelessly create! Thank you for your unwavering support, and for allowing us to turn our dream into a reality.

As you celebrate this event with us, let us share the basic details of our new project. Attached you will find an executive summary for the Broad Street Baking Company, our exciting entry into the lucrative and growing retail bakery/deli café business. As a partner in the BRAVO! L.P., we wish to offer you first right of refusal to participate in the limited partnership of Broad Street prior to any outside solicitations. (We wouldn't want to work with anyone else... we hope the feeling is mutual!)

Again, thank you for your support and encouragement. Our success may never have materialized, if it were not for your involvement.

[Letter sent to limited partners of BRAVO!]

* * *

It was a banner day. BRAVO! had paid off the original 44 investors in three and a half years, much earlier than the five years they predicted it would take. Not only was it a momentous occasion, but also the guys would start drawing more of a salary.

Paying off the investors was Dan's best day: "Paying off BRAVO! getting investors paid out. It was a milestone in my mind. People told us we couldn't do it and we succeeded."

Jeff agrees that this was a monumental day. "The day we made the last payment to investors, we've proven that we can do it."

Linda Kay knew BRAVO! was going to be a success when they started their first payments to investors in the first year, and saw what Dan, Jeff and David were willing to do.

"They took a minimal salary. Their goal was to have a successful restaurant, but also get those investors paid off. And by God they did it. It was fast, and partners have received money just about every year since."

David was thrilled along with his partners, but there were other things causing him to take his eye off the bar at BRAVO!

"I started a family. I was in a band playing music and it started really taking off so my attention was there," David says.

He thought he could be a rock star, even though he now says he was being "delusional" about it. "I was having fun. It was something new for me, so that was exciting," David says.

Working at BRAVO! was a grind that never seemed to let up for him. And he couldn't keep up with Jeff and Dan.

"Dan was more focused on work, and Jeff is very capable of doing a lot of stuff. He'll sit there and work 20-hours straight if that's what it takes. That's just how he operates. Me, I'll work but I also want to do other things," David admits.

His brother noticed the difference in pace. Jeff and Dan were going a "million miles an hour" while David was more laid back.

"His shifts were different. Plus, feeling like the odd man out, it's hard to go the speed we were going, for any amount of time. I was focused and going quickly and that just wasn't in his nature," Dan says.

Dan and his parents all agree that David can do anything he sets his mind to, but as Janice Blumenthal points out: "His pace was totally different from Jeff and Dan's. Three is difficult. Three people working together doesn't work."

Initially when David, Dan and Jeff had considered names for BRAVO!, they looked at Tre Fratelli – three brothers. That brotherhood was about to face its biggest challenge, brought on by Mother Nature.

Photo © Tom and Kasi Beck, all rights reserved

BRAVO! Focaccia

For the dough

4 cups all-purpose flour
2 tablespoons sugar
2 tablespoons salt
½ cup extra virgin olive oil
1 tablespoon instant dry active yeast
2 cups warm water (between 105 and 120 degrees)
For the topping
6 tablespoons extra virgin olive oil
1½ teaspoons kosher salt
1 tablespoon dried oregano

For the dough, place the flour and salt in the mixing bowl or a mixer fitted with a dough hook.

Whisk the oil, yeast and sugar into the warm water. Start the mixer on low speed and immediately pour the water mixture into the bowl.

Mix on low speed for about one minute. Increase the speed slightly and mix for three minutes. Take the bowl off the mixer, cover with a damp towel or plastic wrap and set aside at room temperature to allow the dough to rise, until doubled in size (time will vary, but do not rush it).

When the dough has risen sufficiently, punch it down with your fist.

Prepare a restaurant-spec half-size sheet pan (13 x 18 inches) by spraying it with non-stick coating or greasing it with olive oil. The dough will be wet and can be poured directly into the pan. The dough should spread evenly on the pan to the sides.

For the topping, press your fingertips into the dough, making dimples all over the surface. Pour olive oil over the dough, carefully rubbing it all over the bread. Sprinkle on the salt and oregano.

Preheat oven to 375 degrees.

Allow the bread to rise again at room temperature until the top has risen at least up to the side of the pan [20 – 30 minutes]. Bake in the preheated oven until light brown, turning the pan at least once during the baking process.

Makes 4 large sandwiches

Note from Chef Dan Blumenthal: *This bread is the true backbone of BRAVO! and our other restaurants. It is one of the main table breads at BRAVO!, our most popular sandwich bread and the bread customers crave most. Like all bread making, the process requires patience, but the reward is perfectly fluffy, soft and mouth-watering focaccia.*

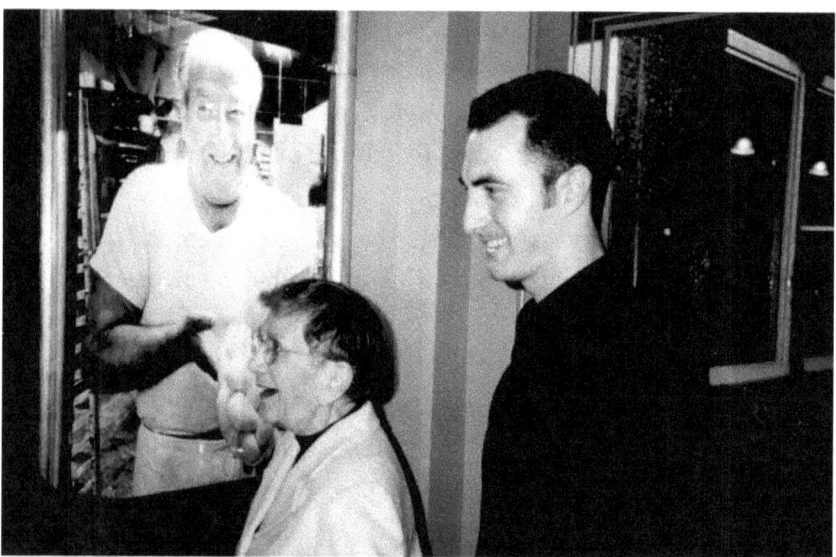
David Blumenthal at Broad Street opening 1998 / photo Dan Blumenthal

CHAPTER 4

THE MIDDLE CHILD

Mississippi awoke to snow on Sunday, December 14, 1997. Several inches covered the ground. In other parts of the country, that little bit of snow wouldn't cause people to bat an eye. But in this part of the world, the entire state practically shuts down for business.

There is no snow removal budget. Jackson doesn't have a legion of snowplows, ready to roll at the first sign of snowflakes. People born in the south certainly don't know how to drive in it, because it's such a rare occurrence. They mostly just wait it out, because they know this sort of weather doesn't last very long, and eventually the sun will come out and melt everything pretty quickly.

But this was no ordinary snow. This was heavy, wet snow—the kind they call "heart attack snow" in the Midwest because it can cause people to keel over while shoveling it. It started falling and continued throughout the morning; eventually more than seven inches would cover the ground in the Jackson metro area.

At BRAVO! the guys were now taking Sundays off, and rotating managerial duties every third week. This Sunday just happened to be David Blumenthal's day in charge. As soon as the employees woke up and looked at the roads, they started calling.

"What do we do? Do we drive into work? Are we going to be open?" David recalls them asking.

There was no "snow plan" in place, because they hadn't had to deal with this since BRAVO! opened three and a half years prior. Several employees were already at the restaurant prepping for the day, so David decided to open on time.

By the end of the lunch "rush," they had only served ten customers. And the nightshift employees were already calling David to find out if they were going to be open that evening. David looked outside at the snow continuing to accumulate on the ground and made the decision to close for the rest of the day.

Around four o'clock in the afternoon, the sun came out, and that meant a lot of the snow started to melt off the roads. The roads would be clear by dinnertime and when people started venturing outside, they headed to BRAVO! only to find it closed. Someone called Dan.

He couldn't believe that BRAVO! was closed, and David hadn't called him. Dan called Jeff to see if he knew about it.

"Did you hear what happened?" Dan asked.

"No."

"Dave closed the restaurant,"

"You're shitting me." Jeff was relatively calm given the news he just heard.

"No, it's true."

It was a shock for them, because neither of them would've closed the restaurant without calling the other partners, and they were both pissed.

"We've never done that before," Jeff said. "We've never made a unilateral decision."

Jeff's anger at David had been building for months and this was just the icing on the cake for him: "I can't imagine what it would be like for Dave to put up with the two of us. But by the same token, he signed up for it."

David admits he made a mistake, but also got mad at them for not trusting him to do the job, after all he was a one-third partner in the business.

"I made the wrong call, in retrospect. I should have consulted with them," David says. "But the other part of that is, had they been there and made that call I probably would've been like 'you were here and it was your call. I trust you to make the right call.' After the snow started melting and the roads were okay it's easy to look back and say 'how could you make that call?'"

David knows they all had a vested interest in the restaurant, both personally and financially, but he felt like the other two partners didn't trust him.

"I think that was an indication to me that there was always a 'big brother' kind of a dynamic. Everybody who's ever had a big brother understands. Or a sibling that's older than you. That knows better than you. That's what older siblings do," David explains.

He had always gotten along with Jeff and Dan, a product of that laid-back personality, but knows discontent had been building between them because of their different working styles. And the snow day was the culmination of that. Especially when closing the restaurant cost them money.

"Every moment you're open is a moment that you could be making money and you have certain fixed costs," David says. "You have certain labor costs and you have staff that has expectations about when they work and how much they work because they depend on making a living. When you close, every day you're closed, your employees aren't making any money and *they* have fixed costs that never go away."

David believes Jeff and Dan were more upset about not consulting them, than about him closing the restaurant itself. Dan agrees with that, calling it a "monumental decision" that would have long-lasting repercussions in the partnership.

"It made a statement that Jeff and I didn't like," Dan says.

"I was bone-headed on my part. But I was young," says David, who was 28 years old at the time of the snow day decision. "The thing was, I was like 'well I'm the boss, why shouldn't I be able to make that decision too?' I was the boss, but I also had two other partners. I should have considered them."

Jeff and Dan were scrutinizing everything David did, especially the way he ordered wine. Ordering wine was a delicate dance. Not only are you dealing with the ABC, but also if you find a vintage you like, you have to place your order months in advance, then wait many more months for it to be ready and to be delivered.

"To push yourself as a place that has a great wine list, a varied selection of wine, you have to pay in Mississippi. You can't just buy a bottle or two. You've got to order a case," David shares.

A lot of times, when David would place a special order, it could be three months before the wine showed up – and even then, it might only be five or six cases. That was on top of his weekly liquor order, which was a set cost in the budget.

"So I would order 20 cases of special order, and the wine would come in at ten thousand dollars," David explains. "That came right out of the account and affected the cash flow."

He would go back and forth with his partners about the wine. They asked him why he ordered so many special order cases.

"I ordered it like six months ago, it's not my fault it came in at one time," he would tell them.

"We had a vision, we knew what we wanted to do and there was synergy there," David says about the beginning days of BRAVO!. But the more they worked together, the more their differences came to light.

"Dan and Jeff are pretty much 'Type A' and I'm not. I'm a 'Type B'. I'm more laid-back. There are no highs or lows with me. I'm a middle child, so I think that has something to do with it. I guess when you're a middle child there's usually chaos above you and chaos below you. You kind of get forgotten," David says.

"I thought we could make it work," Dan says. "He had his own little expertise and he could stay on his side of the fence and we could play well. But there was this sharing that had to go on."

Dan and Jeff didn't sit around and think about it too much, because they had their hands full with the latest restaurant concept: Broad Street Baking Co. This one was going to need much more money to get started.

> **In this mass production world of pre-made, uninspired, quick assembly products, the artisan side of food preparation has been greatly diminished, and with it much of the "soul" of the products.**
>
> As the grandchildren of a second generation baker, as well as owners of one of Jackson's fine dining restaurants, BRAVO!, Dan and David Blumenthal have an appreciation for food quality and product honesty. Along with Jeff Good, this triumvirate, operating through Mangia Bene, Inc., believes that the Metropolitan Jackson market is ready for a food offering which is presently only partly met by existing retail purveyors: a retail bakery and deli café serving fresh old-world artisan breads, pastry (croissants, scones, Danish, muffins, brioche), cookies and cakes. While breads, especially sourdough, will serve as the heart of the business, made-to-order sandwiches, salads, hearty soups and other items will extend the business scope to encompass eat in and take out customers. Corporate box lunch catering, special event catering, pastry and coffee platters, are other components, which will round out the product slate.
>
> The General Partner has chosen Broad Street Baking Company as the name for this venture, in honor of the Blumenthals' grandparents' bakery, which was located on Broad Street in Trenton, New Jersey.
>
> [From the Broad Street Baking Company Private Placement Memorandum]

* * *

Dan, Jeff and David had gone back to the original investors in BRAVO! and pitched them Broad Street. Getting the new restaurant open would take nearly three times the capital it took to open BRAVO!.

When they opened BRAVO!, that was the only thing they had on their plate. They had time to score the concrete floors and build out the kitchen themselves. But renovating the Broad Street space was going to take time, which would take them away from their current restaurant venture, so they planned to hire out the construction.

"BRAVO! in the first rehab, they took that thing apart," Linda Kay Russell recalls. "They put that thing together on a shoestring. All that equipment was used equipment. Whereas when they started Broad Street, they spent a lot more putting it together."

They also decided instead of leasing space for the new café, they were going to be part owners in the building. They had looked at 30 different locations around town and decided on Banner Hall, which was directly across the interstate from BRAVO!.

Banner Hall is built on one of the highest points in Jackson, on the west side of Interstate 55. It's a three-story building that opened in 1986, designed to be an upscale shopping center. But right before it opened, several proposed tenants went out of business, meaning Banner Hall opened under-leased. It had its ups and downs and in 1998, there was an opening where another restaurant had closed.

Two of the other tenants wanted to partner with Mangia Bene to buy the building and the property it sits on. Lemuria, an independent bookstore, had once been housed in Highland Village before moving across the interstate ten years prior; and The Bridal Path/Tuxes Too would be the other partner in Banner Hall LLC – creating a hands-on management team that also had businesses in the building.

The Banner Hall LLC would be able to purchase the building for less than half of what it cost to build and develop originally. It would give them control over their location and provide a second income stream through rent from other tenants.

The price tag to open Broad Street and be part of Banner Hall? One point two million dollars. Jeff, Dan and David planned to sell 80 shares at $15,000 each.

"We invited all of the BRAVO! investors, plus these other people we had met," Dan says of the fundraising for Broad Street.

When they were developing the concept, Dan was adamant that they only do lunch and dinner, and not fuss around with breakfast at Broad Street.

"I never wanted to do breakfast, because I knew what a pain in the ass that was. I knew what it took to get good employees up in the morning and come and do a good product and it was very difficult," Dan says.

David and Jeff overruled Dan on the matter and they designed Broad Street to be open seven days a week, from seven a.m. until eight p.m.

Opening the restaurant would give David some breathing room and time away from Dan and Jeff. He was going to become the General Manager of Broad Street while Jeff stayed at BRAVO! as the General Manager there. Dan would split his time between the two locations with the help of his sous chefs.

Broad Street would be a product-driven restaurant, anchored by the bakery. And they were going to need someone who had artisan baking skills to lead their efforts.

"Artisan baking is a time-honored process which requires skilled workers and very specialized equipment," the Broad Street Baking Company business plan reads. "Artisan baking is an exact science. A master baker must know the chemistry behind the process. It is not baking by recipe."

That person would be Steve Long who had been a baker at BRAVO! and then apprenticed in Nashville at Provence, an artisan bakery and café.

David was looking forward to having his own thing in managing Broad Street, but his brother cautioned him that this was not going to be easy and this business could "eat him up".

"I told my brother, this is a cash business and you have to have very tight controls on this cash, otherwise it will go missing by one of many different ways," Dan said. "Keeping track of the cash in this business is going to drive you crazy."

The biggest issue is the number of transactions that happen each day at Broad Street versus BRAVO!

"At BRAVO! there may be 100 transactions, 100 checks a day," Dan explains. "At Broad Street there may be a thousand a day, because every person that goes up to that register, that's a transaction. That's a payment. That's an order."

These days, those transactions are more credit card-driven, with less cash changing hands. But in the beginning, it was mostly all cash, and Dan knew managing just the cash would be a full-time job.

Dan recalled his days at the Boudin Sourdough French Bread Café in San Francisco.

"All that cash has to be accounted for. I've been there. I've done that. I've lived that. I knew that Broad Street would be two or three times the amount of transactions that I'd done just because of the size of it."

The cash would only be part of the challenge at Broad Street.

"Then all the little intricacies of baking everything from scratch had its own complexities," Dan goes on. "You're running breakfast, lunch and dinner through a kitchen. You're baking bread and you're baking pastries on site. You've got all these worker bees that are bumping into each other and you're having to manage them."

Dan warned David that Broad Street would have a lot of moving parts and would be a lot of work, but David said he was up for the challenge and began working on the Broad Street build-out with Jeff and Dan.

Getting Broad Street up and running would take them out of BRAVO! and customers had become accustomed to seeing the three partners when they came to dine there. BRAVO! was a personality-driven restaurant, and without the personalities, what was it?

Lesley Tolar had been promoted to bar manager at BRAVO! and fielded a lot of questions about Jeff, Dan and David.

"When they opened Broad Street they just disappeared. I mean they were just gone," Lesley says.

"BRAVO! had a hard time when they opened Broad Street," Linda Kay adds. "People expected to see Jeff in there. People love BRAVO!, not just for BRAVO! They loved it and a huge part of it was seeing Jeff in there."

They also had to start hiring people to help manage and do day-to-day operations at BRAVO!

"When Jeff and me and Dave were running it, we were a strong team. We could do it with the best of them. I really didn't have much doubt," Dan remembers. "When we started hiring people to do our jobs as we grew the thing, that's when you have a little more doubt, because you're trusting other people to do things. You're delegating things."

And how do you train someone else to have the level of trust and care that you have as a founder? The guys found it's much harder than they thought. But it all started with their principles of customer service.

"Every transaction has to be the same to the same level, whether it's a call center, whether it's a cash register driven service counter, or whether it's a more complex transaction like a doctor's office," Jeff says. "You've got to realize that every transaction is new to that customer, although it may be the twentieth for you that day."

They were teaching that to their teams at BRAVO! and to their new team at Broad Street, who would eventually open the restaurant right in the middle of the busiest season of the year.

* * *

Upon entering, customers will follow "Broad Street" – a faux cobblestone path to the central counter where they will be greeted. Guests will be able to select from an abundance of fresh bread and pastry to eat on site or take out. Actual product will surround the customer. Menu items (sandwiches, soups, salads, light entrees) can be ordered from the menu and prepared quickly.

If ordering from the menu, the customer's order will be taken and their drinks and ready-to-serve items will be immediately

assembled. They will pay their bill, be given a service number and offered the chance to be seated at a table, booth or counter. As each customer's order is completed, service attendants will bring the orders directly to the customer's tables and remove any unwanted items at this time.

Unlike fast foods, one does not wait for the food to be placed on a tray, yet unlike full-service restaurants the number of personnel, and amount of time and expense of taking an order and serving the order, are reduced.

[From "A Service Walk-through at Broad Street Baking Company" in the Broad Street Baking Company Business Plan]

* * *

The Broad Street Baking Company opened for business on Friday, December 11, 1998 and it was swamped from day one.

"You try not to open a restaurant during Christmas season," Dan says. "We got hammered. It's busy enough to open a restaurant, and then if you open it during the busiest season of the year, you're just asking for trouble in my mind."

When they opened BRAVO! they were relatively unknown to the marketplace, and the food would take a while to catch on. By the time they opened the doors at Broad Street, they had a built-in customer base at BRAVO! that was ready to see what they had to offer.

"Broad Street quickly turned out to be a Jackson landmark," David says. "People know it from everywhere, it's such a great place to go."

Walking into Broad Street Baking Company, you notice the large gallery-style pictures hanging on the wall. There are pictures of Sol and Deborah Blumenthal, David and Dan's grandparents, and the Blumenthals' bakery on Broad Street in Trenton, New Jersey. In every photo, Sol is wearing his baking shirt and a great big smile. You get the sense that he worked all the time, but loved every single minute of it.

When they unlock the doors and open the gates at seven o'clock in the morning, the regular customers are waiting to place their coffee and breakfast orders. Employees at the counter know everyone by name and greet the regulars with a smile and sometimes a joke.

Within a half hour, the place fills up with business people having a breakfast meeting; entrepreneurs taking advantage of the free Wi-Fi and free coffee refills as they put together proposals on their laptops; and moms who just dropped the kids off at school, grabbing something to go before they head to their next stop. During election season you'll find candidates for every position under the sun walking around, sharing their platforms and shaking hands with people in the crowd. The place will stay packed through the lunch rush and well into the afternoon.

The smell of fresh baking bread and pastries is a constant inside Broad Street, and your mouth is already watering as you read the descriptions on the menu. Everything is made from scratch; there's not a mix to be found in the kitchen.

"All of the muffins, croissants, Danish, all those get done at four a.m. so they come out hot," Dan explains the baking schedule. "The bread baking gets done at night and at this point they start about two o'clock in the afternoon and goes to about midnight."

If it's your first time at Broad Street, you might get decision paralysis. There are so many great items to choose from.

"We opened Broad Street and it was a handful," David says. "It's probably the most difficult of these businesses to run because of the product line they offer. The amount of different things; you've got pastries, cookies, cakes and breads, all this stuff. It's incredibly labor-intensive and takes a lot of energy and a lot of money to make."

They also realized having a café to go along with the bakery was creating problems in the kitchen.

"We made a blunder in making the bakery so big physically and not leaving enough room for the kitchen to service a very busy deli," Jeff says.

Then they started to notice Broad Street wasn't making the profit they thought it would.

"Broad Street has always been a business that makes a dollar, spends a dollar. It doesn't matter how much we make, it's going to be a dollar in, a dollar out," Jeff explains.

A lot of those dollars "out" were in labor costs.

"Broad Street has so many employees," Linda Kay shares. "It's so complicated. It's so expensive to run. In the service industry, the customer pays your servers [through tips]."

That's not the case at Broad Street because it's not a full-service restaurant. The business has to pay cashiers two and a half times the typical server wage. There is a tip jar, which the employees split, but those tips aren't in line with the 20 percent you might see at BRAVO! Plus, there's only so much you can charge for your bakery products. The profit margin is razor-thin.

"Bread is not cheap [to make], but you can't sell bread for a whole lot," Linda Kay says. "It's one of the big selling points of the place, the fresh pastries. I don't know how a bakery alone does it."

"I have a great love for Broad Street, but BRAVO! is my favorite," Buddy Blumenthal shares. "Broad Street, I should have a great attraction to because so much of my family is involved in that. My father, mother. But it's a concept that was a failure to begin with and they've made it work. So it breaks even but it will never be a moneymaker."

Dan's prophecies about the business eating him up were coming back to haunt David.

"I was working over there [starting at] five a.m.," David remembers. "Coming in to Bravo at nine a.m. was a breeze compared to going over to Broad Street at five and opening the place up. That just kind of wore me down."

And that was taking its toll on his personal life, as he was in the middle of getting a divorce.

"I worked so much I think I single-handedly wrecked my marriage. I was at a time in my life where I felt like I needed a break. I was strung very thin."

It hadn't escaped the notice of Jeff and Dan.

Right after opening Broad Street, Jeff and Debbie Good took their first vacation together in years. On the long plane ride back from Europe,

Jeff started thinking about all the hard work he had put in to raising the capital for Broad Street and all of the things that still needed to be done at the restaurants, especially on David's end. He wrote it all down in a lengthy memo to David.

"It was cathartic," Jeff says now. "I was so mad. I felt so wronged. Before email, I memo'ed him to death."

Dan noticed his brother's mind had begun to wander.

"It was just him doing the same job and he's thinking he's doing fine," Dan says. "Jeff and I step in and say 'you're not performing.' He wasn't giving 100 percent."

David agreed and would be gone by the time Broad Street celebrated its first anniversary.

* * *

> **You have asked for it, so we are going to give it to you!!! Catering has been one of the better kept secrets at BRAVO!, but with the addition of Broad Street, we are coming out of the closet. We are launching a completely separate "division" that will do nothing but cater.**
>
> **On-site dinners, high-end cocktail parties, corporate box lunch catering, or decorated take out party platters; we are launching an effort to provide full catering services to our customer base.**
>
> **[From "The Bravo Buzz" Fall/Winter 1998]**

* * *

When David Blumenthal was kindergarten age, he decided one day he just wasn't going back to school.

"I remember trying to get David in the car to go to kindergarten and we didn't live far from the school," Janice says.

This is when they were living in Pennsylvania, and she called Buddy in Philadelphia telling him he had to "come home now." Janice couldn't get David to budge.

"David, what's the problem honey? Why won't you go to school?" Janice asked him.

"I don't like the crossing guard," David replied. "The crossing guard's mean."

Buddy came home, and loaded David into the cargo area in the back of their station wagon. He drove to the school and straight to the outside door of the classroom.

"I opened the door of the station wagon and shoved him through," Buddy remembers. "I don't know what the hell the teacher was thinking."

"Buddy's the disciplinarian," Janice adds.

This wasn't their first struggle with getting David to go to school.

"The year before we had him in a Montessori school and he loved Montessori school," Buddy says. "Once he started kindergarten he was going to the same school Dan was going to. Dan was three grades ahead and he was so proud."

"I'm going to Dan's school," David would say.

"Well, you'll go to Dan's school in the morning and the Montessori school in the afternoon," Buddy reminded him.

After three days of kindergarten, David came home and announced: "I'm not going back to that baby school anymore. I'm going to the big person's school where Dan goes."

So they pulled him out of Montessori school, and not long after that was the refusal to go to kindergarten because of the crossing guard. But that only lasted about a week.

"David didn't like structure," Janice says. "And he's that way to this day. Jon was like that. They like to do what they want to do, when they want to do it."

"Jon was very free form," Buddy agrees.

Maybe Jon, the youngest Blumenthal brother, could see the writing on the wall between Dan and David. Maybe it was something David said to him. Whatever the catalyst, Jon came to David with a business opportunity at the start of 1999.

"Jon approached me about helping him put together a business. First he told me what he wanted to do, and we sat down and I helped him run through some numbers," David says they were trying to figure out if it would be a viable business.

"We went through the numbers and I was like: I can make a whole lot more money doing that than I can in the restaurant business," David realized. "And it's less time."

It was an open MRI business that would have an outpatient imaging center. He saw it as a way to get his life back, working fewer hours and no longer working nights, weekends and holidays. David had been through the opening of a business with BRAVO! and Broad Street. He felt that if he could make it through that initial phase of trying to get the business off the ground, things would be easier.

"I might not have to work 70, 80 hours a week and I could make a lot more money doing it," David thought.

He went to Dan and Jeff and said he wanted out of the partnership.

"The truth of the matter is, when Dave went to Broad Street I knew it was going to crash," Dan says. "Dave can do anything he puts his mind to but Broad Street was a beast that was going to just eat everybody. Adding on top of that, ensuring that it would suck the life out of us, is trying to push it forward to success. Broad Street is a Swiss watch. There are thousands of moving parts and if one of them goes wrong, or doesn't synchronize, the whole thing doesn't work."

Jeff and Dan came to an agreement to buy David out of his part of the business. A buyout was part of their partnership agreement, and it would take Jeff and Dan three years to pay David out.

"You had a pie that was divided three ways and even though he wasn't necessarily doing one-third of the work, he was getting paid one-third the money. When he left, it really hurt because you went from having three people to do the job, to two people," Dan says.

When they completed the buyout, there would be more financial rewards for Dan and Jeff, but that was bittersweet. And it's the biggest regret of Dan's business life.

"The partnership that we originally had, to split up the way it did," Dan says. "The relationship with David was strained after that. It took a bunch of years, but is strained even to this day. Anytime you talk about business, it takes him right back."

David says the whole thing was a great learning experience and he has this advice to anyone who wants to open a restaurant: "Obviously you've got to work hard. But you also have to keep life in perspective. You have to realize that there is more to life than work and money. Time will pass you by and before you know it, you don't have those opportunities to have a family. Take care of yourself. Make time for your family. Don't make work the center of your universe because you can't take it with you when you die."

Tuesday, August 31, 1999 marked David's last day as manager and partner in BRAVO! and Broad Street.

* * *

> **Welcome to Robert Gardner, General Manager of Broad Street Baking Company.**
>
> **Robert comes to us as no stranger. Dan and Jeff met Robert when he was working with Pavailler of America – the domestic marketing group for the French baking equipment manufacturer of the same name. Robert assisted us in designing our baking center, and actually "moved in with us" for the first few weeks we were open, helping the Broad Street baking and pastry departments perfect their processes as we learned to use highly specialized European baking equipment.**
>
> **[From "The Dish" newsletter from Mangia Bene, Spring/Summer 2000]**

* * *

"Robert ended up coming to work with us and took David's place as G.M.," Jeff says. "One of the first things he said was: 'something's got to happen, your kitchen's not big enough. You won't have enough room to operate here.' We needed more room for the kitchen."

Robert pitched the idea of creating a wholesale baking arm to Broad Street. They could move the baking operations off site from Banner Hall, and not only bake bread and pastries for their two restaurants, but for other restaurants in the area as well.

It was an ambitious plan that they were all excited about. Jeff was ready to plow full steam ahead, without thinking through some of the drawbacks to the plan. He just *hoped* it would all work out; something Dan and Jeff both refer to as "smoking hope-ium."

"So we all smoke 'hope-ium' and we decide we're going to do this, move everything and just put everything back together," Jeff says. "Now we're breaking it all down and moving it to a new place and putting it back together. It forever changed Broad Street."

They now had two locations with two sets of overhead. Then there is the matter of timing. You couldn't just pull the fresh bread or cookies out of the oven and put them on the racks out front to sell anymore. They had to bake things way in advance in order for them to have time to cool off, be packed and trucked to their final destinations.

"By coming up with new ways to create revenue, which is to sell things wholesale, which is to sell things at 50 percent off retail as a starting point, is a loss for us, because we never could get the volume where it needed to be," Jeff says.

They had all sorts of trouble with the venture. For starters, their main bakers left not long after they opened the wholesale bakery. Then, there was the issue of the restaurateurs who weren't used to seeing fresh bread the way Broad Street made it.

"I remember trying to sell po'boy bread and this guy held out forever because he wanted the New Orleans po'boy bread, stuff baked a week ago that comes in bags and you keep it in your freezer," Dan remembers. "We baked a damn good po'boy bread. It didn't look exactly like the other and it was a little larger. He started buying it and we thought we were really a hit because he does good business."

Their dreams of selling 500 loaves a week to this particular restaurant were dashed when the owner decided he didn't want to deal with fresh bread.

"He's so used to pulling it from the freezer," Dan says.

"And nobody's paying their bills," Jeff adds. "We're baking bread ahead of time and delivering and they say 'we don't want that.'"

It was another strike for Broad Street. And if it made no profit, Dan and Jeff didn't get paid. The Limited Partnership for Broad Street was different than BRAVO!, Dan and Jeff received a percentage of sales.

"I used to have a real hate relationship with Broad Street," Dan says. "Nothing was easy. Everything was a struggle. Jeff and I get a percentage of sales over there, and when things get bad the first people not to get paid is us."

It's something they didn't have to do, because in the Broad Street Limited Partnership agreement, they were entitled to receive their management fee, which is a percentage of the topline revenue. But they knew they could bankrupt the business doing that.

"We'd go months without getting a paycheck," Dan adds. "So you build up resentment."

"As we're losing all this money, I came up with the brilliant idea to open another retail outlet so there's a place to sell more retail," Jeff said.

When they were scouting locations for Broad Street and BRAVO!, they looked for places with ease of access (close to their projected customer base), safety, co-located businesses and popularity (lots of people might go there).

Downtown Jackson was ruled out in both cases:

"Downtown Jackson is only viable for lunch business," the Broad Street Baking Company business plan reads.

"Perhaps after further downtown development occurs it would be a viable choice, but not at this time," comes from the BRAVO! business plan.

By 2002, there hadn't been significant development downtown. There weren't a lot of other businesses nearby, but Jeff pushed for it after suggestions from their customers.

"Jeff was trying to please too many people. People would say 'why don't y'all come downtown?' That doesn't mean it's a good idea because one person wants to do it," Dan says.

They ended up renovating a building on the corner of Capitol and President Streets and turning it into a Broad Street Express. It was not far from the state capitol and other state government buildings. Plus, there were several professional buildings with many employees located downtown.

"The idea was it would be grab and go," Jeff explains. "A quick nosh, a quick sandwich place."

Problem was, this "quick" sandwich place had no place to sit. Customers would come into Broad Street Express, get their order, and be sent out the back door. In downtown Jackson, there are very few people who are willing to eat outside on a bench in the boiling heat of summer.

"We failed immensely by not having a dining room," Jeff admits.

That's now three Broad Street ventures that weren't doing well.

"That was doing so swimmingly well losing so much money we decided to do a second location downtown because we were offered free space," Jeff says shaking his head.

They had all sorts of trouble with the venture.

The owners of the second downtown location offered to renovate the space for them, if Broad Street would just pay rent. The guys agreed and opened their second downtown location in 2003.

"We opened one Broad Street Express downtown that was marginal, so why not do another one?" Dan laughs. "The goal at that time was to push revenue and get revenue to a certain level. We were trying to grow our way out of revenue problems. It made sense on paper, but really if one wasn't doing well, why would the other one do well?"

It too failed.

"It wouldn't do any volume. They're losing four to five hundred dollars a day each, just because of payroll," Jeff said.

In 2004, Dan called a meeting with Jeff. They had been business partners for a little more than a decade, and best friends longer than that, but this Broad Street debacle was about to test both of those relationships.

Jeff walked into Dan's office and found him sitting behind the desk. Usually the two joke around with each other, but not this day. Dan was wearing a serious look on his face and got right to the point.

"I just want to let you know, I've talked to a lawyer. I know if we declare bankruptcy, I can keep my car and I can keep my house. I'm ready to do that," Dan started. "I don't know what you and Debbie want to do, but I'm ready to declare bankruptcy."

Jeff sat in an uncharacteristic silence.

"You need to fix this or we're going to declare bankruptcy," Dan said.

"All he had to do was be very stern with me and recalibrate this squirrel brain I've got. He held me accountable for the problem that we had and he pushed me on it because I was the one who said we needed to be downtown," Jeff says of the meeting.

He cleared everything from his schedule and completely focused on getting out from under both of the downtown restaurants. Jeff found someone to take over the leases. All of the equipment and renovations on the Capitol Street building were left behind. Broad Street Express closed their downtown locations in 2004.

They were still stuck with the offsite wholesale bakery. A very "Jackson" problem at Banner Hall would soon create an opportunity to set things right.

* * *

From: Gail Jones
Subject: Foundation Meeting
Date: September 8, 2008

Good Afternoon!
There will be a meeting of the partners this Thursday, September 11th at 2 p.m. at Banner Hall to discuss the foundation issues and the recommended fix. Jim Moss of J.A. Moss Construction and Britt Maxwell, structural engineer, will be attending. Jeff is contacting Michael Boerner of Barranco Architects regarding attending this meeting. He is doing the restroom drawings.

It appears there has been some fairly significant movement on the Broad Street side of the building over the last couple of months necessitating the need to go ahead and have the foundation work done just as soon as it is reasonably possible.

-Email from the manager of Banner Hall about foundation issues

* * *

The crack started small, barely noticeable at first. Then, it grew a little longer. And a little longer until it ran the entire length of the north dining room at Broad Street Baking Company in Banner Hall.

The problem? Yazoo clay.

Yazoo clay is expansive clay found only in this part of Mississippi. It's called "Yazoo clay" because of its outcropping along the Yazoo River Basin. The U.S. Army Corps of Engineers did an intense study of it in 1969 and released a report saying: "swelling and shrinkage of soils are responsible for considerable damages to buildings and other structures in many parts of the world. One of these regions is in Jackson, Mississippi and the surrounding area, where many types of structures have been damaged from movements of the underlying Yazoo clay formation."

Yazoo clay moves and often takes a building or a road with it. The report found some cases of structural displacements that were as much as one foot. And sidewalk "heaves" of nearly five inches.

There are homes in Jackson where closet or bedroom doors won't shut all the way, cracks appear on walls, or the sidewalk out front is buckled. Sometimes it's tree roots. Other times it's Yazoo clay. The majority of foundation problems in the Jackson area are caused by Yazoo clay and fixing it is expensive. If you buy or sell property in this area now, Yazoo clay is a required disclosure. The best way to know for sure, is to hire an inspector and get the ground tested.

Engineers tested the ground underneath Banner Hall and not only found Yazoo clay, but also the damage it already had caused.

"There was movement and beams were broken and they decided they needed to go fix that," Dan says.

The engineers came back and told Dan and Jeff that the only way they could fix the Banner Hall clay problem was to excavate, right under their dining room.

Dan couldn't believe the news: "I just remember shaking my head and asking 'how are we going to survive that one?'"

Going in through the north dining room would mean a complete shutdown of that side of the restaurant. They wouldn't have access to several tables, the express takeout counter – or the restrooms.

Jeff got real creative with how they would handle it and brought the entire team together for a staff meeting on February 25, 2009.

"A Hotty Toddy port-a-potty will be rolled into place this weekend and will become our guest restrooms! These are top-flight, heated or air conditioned units with running water and complete facilities," Jeff told the staff.

He also told them they were going to make lemonade out of the lemons, by going to full-service.

"It was one of those things that maybe this provided an opportunity for us to try something different, to go full-service. From a numbers standpoint it could be positive," Dan says.

And since the restaurant was going to be ripped apart anyway, this was the perfect time to bring the bakery back in house at Banner Hall.

"We said okay if that happened then we need to add on to the building and bring the bakery back," Jeff says.

Jeff and Dan laid out the remodeling plan from the wait stations to the service line to the dining room layout. They worked out where the offices would move. They detailed the upgrades and what would be closed and how they would handle it. Jeff offered suggestions to the staff members on how to handle customer questions and complaints.

"They figured out how to run the restaurant with only half the building," Buddy Blumenthal says. "They both worked on it. If they're working on it together it doesn't make any difference, they're like Siamese twins."

On Sunday, March first, they shut down the restaurant as it was, and then followed Jeff's punch list to get everything ready for construction to start the next day. They changed all the service lines. They cut electrical and data lines to the affected areas. They sealed off the area for the construction and hoped it wouldn't take forever to fix.

"All that was shut down with porta-potties in the parking lot for months," Jeff remembers. "They removed the windows and brought in a backhoe."

The engineers planned to go through the floor in Broad Street to get to the foundation underneath Banner Hall. They would then hand-excavate the Yazoo clay with buckets, and repair any damage.

It didn't take long for them to find another problem. Engineers found that the slab was a 12-inch structural slab poured on Styrofoam and only reinforced on the bottom.

An email from the construction team reads: "The slab is definitely more difficult to remove and it is certainly much heavier. We estimate the added weight of the concrete and steel is 40,000 pounds to 60,000 pounds more than that shown on the original drawings. Our best options are to use a breaker on the end of our Bobcat or to saw cut the slab. Both ways require approximately the same costs, but saw cutting will be completed faster and without the dust and vibration problems."

Jeff wondered out loud if the building was cursed and Dan worried about how it was going to affect their bottom line. Some customers stayed away because of construction. Others wouldn't go in because of the change to full-service.

"Customers hated that because they wanted to have the freedom of how they ordered," Jeff explains.

Construction and renovations took months, and they lost a half a million dollars in business. That was down 20 percent for the year.

* * *

Dear Broad Street Limited Partner:

Attached, please find your K-1 for your investment in Broad Street Baking Company, L.P. for the 2009 tax year. It is with great relief that we announce that we have weathered what has been our worst year ever operationally and our second-worst year financially. The damage to our business brought about from the foundation repair project starting the first week of March and lasting until the first week of October was profound. Our business fell off 20% the day the construction started. We lost half of our main dining room, our take out counter, half of our register counter area and our bathrooms.

The positive that came out of the construction process was the addition we made to our space. We leveraged the construction crew and the turmoil that was happening in our space and parking lot by adding on to our kitchen in such a way as to provide the necessary space to allow us to bring our bakery back on site from its near decade-long "exile" at the Cabot Lodge Millsaps. We closed down the first weekend in October and made the move.. and in four days we moved figurative mountains. We reopened with a new front counter setup, new bathrooms, new patio/outdoor seating, new couches and soft seating upstairs and a fully integrated kitchen and bakery...just like it was back in 1998 when we started this journey!

In order to fund this project, Dan and Jeff took out a personally guaranteed loan for $400,000. As the General Partners to this venture, it is our responsibility to do the hard things that must be done to ensure its survival. In addition, Dan and Jeff ceased taking their contractual management fee on July 2, 2009. Sacrifice was the word of the day, and there was no way that anything other than sacrifice could be made throughout the balance of 2009 into 2010.

We want you to be proud of our restaurant and proud of us. We will not stop until you are.

[Broad Street Baking Company L.P. Annual Report 2009]

* * *

Broad Street bounced back from the 2009 construction. When the restaurant reopened afterwards, they went back to counter service. Jeff and Dan also decided it was time for a marketing blitz.

"We made a big scene of it and things came back pretty quick," Dan recalls. "We switched back to the old service and people were happy. It kind of says something about what they like about that concept. They sort of enjoy the way it works."

It would take Dan and Jeff another eight years to pay off the loans for Broad Street. They made the final payment in October, 2017. They were also able to finally pay off the loan to purchase Banner Hall. It was great news they couldn't wait to share with the investors.

* * *

Dear Broad Street Limited Partner:
We have some exciting news for you! (You might want to sit down before reading any further!) WE ARE THRILLED TO ANNOUNCE THAT WE ARE MAKING A CASH DISTRIBUTION FOR THE FIRST TIME SINCE 2010!
As usual, Dan Blumenthal and Jeff Good, working through their General Partner entity Mangia Bene, Inc. are foregoing their contracted share of the distribution in order to accelerate the return capital to the Limited Partners. It is the intent of the General Partner to return 100% of each Limited Partner's initial $15,000 before taking any portion of the contractual 35% earned share of cash distributions.
We have worked our way through catastrophes like the foundation problem, an outflow of population to the suburbs and more recently the on-going issues with reliable water supply which results in multiple boil water notices a year and sometimes outright closedowns due to no water service at all.
-Broad Street Baking Company, L.P. Annual Report 2017

* * *

Broad Street Baking Company continues to be a dollar for dollar business, as it goes after the elusive dinner crowd. Dan and Jeff have talked about only keeping it open for breakfast and lunch, and closing it in the afternoon. But they do enough business after three o'clock, it makes sense to keep it open.

"It still has to be open because we have to be baking and doing things," Dan says. "And nobody likes to throw in the towel. We're not the only fast casual concept that has the same problem."

They've tried dinner specials. They offer beer and wine for sale. In 2017, Broad Street started "burger night" on Thursday nights. There would be a special burger offered every Thursday, and it caught on quickly. It was so popular, the burgers would sell out every time. So, they expanded "burger night" to every night of the week, after four p.m. But that's still not the missing link to make Broad Street more profitable.

"We're still searching for the holy grail of dinner business. Jeff and I think there is a magic spot there somewhere that if we do something, we'll pick up," Dan shares.

He continues to work on the menu and work with Jeff on the marketing of the restaurant because it has to stick around.

"Financially, Broad Street has been a mixed bag, because we still have investors out there that we owe a lot of money to," Dan explains. "There is still the feeling that it's not the success that it needs to be."

The real estate helps ease some of that pressure, because if Banner Hall were ever to sell, all of the investors would walk away with a piece of the profits. Dan has made his peace with Broad Street, but still refers to it as a "troubled child." It's the troubled middle child in their restaurant family. In 2007, Dan and Jeff developed a third restaurant concept that would attract attention outside of Jackson, Mississippi. And this time, they would put their own money on the line.

Field greens salad with Balsamic Vinaigrette
Photo © Tom and Kasi Beck, all rights reserved

BRAVO! Balsamic Vinaigrette

¾ cup aged balsamic vinegar
¼ cup water
¾ tablespoon garlic, minced
1 tablespoon Zatarain's creole mustard
2 tablespoons plus 1 scant teaspoon sugar
2 teaspoons dry Italian seasoning
1 teaspoon ground black pepper
1 teaspoon salt
2 cups olive oil

Place all ingredients except for the olive oil in a food processor or blender. Turn on the processor or blender and slowly pour in the olive oil until the vinaigrette thickens and is fully emulsified.

Makes about 3 cups

Note from Chef Dan Blumenthal: *This balsamic vinaigrette is another backbone in my culinary repertoire, and is used to best effect these days as a staple for our mixed greens salad at Broad Street. Another customer favorite, it has many uses, including as a great marinade for grilled vegetables.*

Left to right, Jon Pixler, Maggie Brown, Jeff Good, Rebecca Lacey (Biloxi Sal & Mookie's), Bruce Lacey (Biloxi Sal & Mookie's), Dan Blumenthal (photo courtesy Dan Blumenthal)

CHAPTER 5

DO THE RIGHT THING

The youngest "child" in the Mangia Bene family was born out of a craving for pizza and ice cream. Dan Blumenthal has loved pizza for as long as he can remember and learned to really make it well when he was working in San Francisco.

When he started with Spuntino in 1989, the company sent him to train at its sister restaurant, Prego. That's where he learned to make Neapolitan style pizza, which is governed by the very strict rules of the Associazione Verace Pizza Napoletana in Italy. The products you use to make your pizza must come from the Campania region of Italy. The pizza must be "made from a base of risen dough and cooked in a wood-fired oven" and should be "soft, elastic and easy to manipulate and fold" when it's cooked. And there are rules about the water, salt and ingredients.

Dan discovered one of his strengths in the kitchen was pizza.

So in 2006, when the Broad Street downtown mess was sorted out,

Dan started thinking about opening a new concept altogether: a restaurant that specialized in pizza, where you could sit down and eat it with your friends and family.

"It was a huge market that I saw was underserved. When you went and opened the yellow pages and looked at who was doing pizza, it was all fast food delivery," Dan says.

Dan went to Jeff and told him he had an idea for a new concept but: "We're not doing anything until we identify six managerial-type people that we can take out of BRAVO! without damaging our operation."

He wanted Jeff to pick three people from the front of the house, and he would pick three from the back of the house. When they had their lists, they started talking concept.

Jeff also wanted to do something family-friendly – an ice cream parlor. One of their BRAVO! customers was considering starting a franchise for Ben and Jerry's. Dan suggested they open a co-branded restaurant. The pizza on one side, Ben and Jerry's on the other. It would be the first Ben and Jerry's in Mississippi.

Jeff argued against that: "We can control it better and make more revenue if we do it ourselves."

They kicked around ideas for a few months, but nothing ever caught traction until one night when Dan watched the Spike Lee film *Do The Right Thing*.

He knew exactly what their new restaurant should be called: Sal & Mookie's, after the two main characters in the movie. It also sparked the idea to have a New York style pizza joint. The décor would be "old world" with red-checkered tablecloths, but the pizza would have "new world" gourmet ingredients and fun names. Dan would also add burgers, pasta, paninis and sub sandwiches to the menu.

"This is the one that will travel," Dan said of the concept. "We could do these things all over the country. Sal & Mookie's would work anywhere."

Jeff knew of the perfect location. Fondren was an up-and-coming neighborhood in Jackson, just to the north of the booming hospital corridor that was being built along State Street and Woodrow Wilson Boulevard. There was a building that had once been a restaurant, before a kitchen fire gutted it.

"That part of Fondren had seen a rise and fall," Dan says. "We got good rent on the building, but we would have to put a lot of money into it."

The concept started coming together quickly and they had found a location. Now they needed to convince their six restaurant leaders to move to the new location. Most of them had been working at BRAVO! for several years, like Jon Pixler who had worked his way up from cook to sous chef, and was proud of it.

"If people asked me where I work, I would say 'I work at BRAVO!'. My chest pokes out a little bit because everyone always says 'I love that place!' I bled BRAVO! I *was* BRAVO!," Pixler says.

Dan called him into the office and told him: "We're thinking about opening a new concept, a pizza concept and we want you to be the chef."

"No. I'm not interested," Pixler said without a moment's hesitation.

"Okay," Dan said and Pixler thought that was the end of it. But he hadn't gotten the pitch from uber-salesman Jeff yet.

"We just knew he had energy and drive and if we could cheerlead him, he could get behind a project," Dan says now. "On paper it maybe didn't seem as good as what he was doing. He was working in one of the best restaurants in Jackson and he had a good system. Things were going pretty well. Why would he jump?"

A day or two later, Jeff asked Pixler to meet him and Dan at the burned out restaurant in Fondren. The kitchen fire hadn't just gutted the inside of the building, there were spots that had no roof; you could see blue sky right over your head.

Dan and Jeff explained the concept of Sal & Mookie's and walked Pixler through what that would look like. They told him what a valuable asset he was and how they needed a leader here. But Pixler still said no.

A few days later, Jeff picked Pixler up and drove him to the burned out building. Instead of going back in, Jeff asked him to sit on the grass on the other side of Taylor Street, which ran next to the restaurant.

"I want you to imagine this patio, full of kids and their parents having ice cream, and what that would mean to the City of Jackson... to have a family concept like this, in this part of town," Jeff began. "This is an amazing idea and we need to do this for our city. But Jon, this can't happen without you."

Third time was a charm. Pixler said yes.

"He's Jeff Good. You can't tell him no," Pixler says. "It was very emotional leaving BRAVO! for me because there was so much personal growth in that building."

The other five also needed the concept "walk-through" at Sal & Mookie's before they said yes.

When they opened BRAVO! Jeff didn't have the money to eat at every one of the competitive restaurants for market analysis. This time would be different. Jeff, Debbie and Dan took a trip to New York City to really experience "New York Style" pizza. They ate so much pizza, they were practically sick of it. In four days, they had been to 18 pizza joints in the Big Apple. They wrapped up a dozen samples to bring back on the plane for Pixler, because he refused to fly.

Jeff and Pixler would lead the build-out of Sal & Mookie's but before construction got started, Dan wanted a number. How much was this going to cost?

"It's going to be like a house remodel," Jeff said. "We'll get a contractor and I can't imagine it would be more than $400,000."

In 1993 when they were opening BRAVO! no bank would give them a loan, so they sold shares. They did that again with Broad Street. But this time, Jeff and Dan were going to own the restaurant outright. They took their idea to the bank and got a small business loan, without having to produce a business plan.

That decision would haunt them for years to come.

* * *

Construction was underway on the Sal & Mookie's location in Fondren. The brand new stainless steel kitchen equipment had arrived and was ready to be installed. The construction crew was refurbishing the burned out part of the restaurant and building a new dining room with a brick floor.

For every brick that went into the floor, it cost one dollar to be installed. When it was finished, Jeff looked at the floor. The bricks were covered in mortar that hadn't been wiped off when it was wet, now it had hardened to the surface. Mortar is made up of cement and isn't easily cleaned up.

"Why didn't you clean up the bricks when you laid them down?" Jeff asked the contractor.

"Because that costs extra. Do you want us to clean that off for you?" the contractor replied.

Jeff was trying to be mindful of the costs and told him no, then asked: "But how do you clean it off?"

The contractor told him to use muriatic acid.

Muriatic acid is another term for hydrochloric acid. It can be super helpful if you're trying to clean stone or brick and nothing else works. But it's also incredibly corrosive to metals and the human body. It can cause severe burns on your skin and in your lungs if you breathe it in. Even Bob Vila calls it a "last resort" when doing home improvement.

The contractor told Jeff to dilute it then use it to clean the bricks. Jeff bought one case of muriatic acid – that had four gallons inside. He diluted the acid in a mop bucket. Jeff and his team went to work, trying to clean up the mortar. They were unsuccessful.

The next day, Jeff bought two cases of the acid, respirators and wire brushes. He rented a floor buffer. Then, the team set out again to clean up the floor. They took turns in the dining room, putting undiluted muriatic acid on the bricks and scrubbing it with the wire brushes and buffer. The fumes were strong, even with the construction-grade respirators they were wearing, but they were making progress, getting the floor cleaned.

When Jeff arrived the next morning, he couldn't believe his eyes. The surface of the brand-new stainless steel kitchen equipment had turned black from the muriatic acid fumes. The oven. The hoods. The refrigerators. Everything.

Jeff and his team took Comet and green scrubby sponges and went over every inch of stainless steel surface in the restaurant, until they cleaned off the black film. Dan says it took "forever" to get the smell out of the restaurant.

Other projects were going better – building a walk-in cooler, creating a window for kids to be able to watch pizzas being made, constructing a huge deck and installing landscaping outside. But the project was running over budget. Way over budget.

"Every three weeks I'd go to Dan and say 'I think we need to go borrow more money,'" Jeff recalls.

"There were very strong disagreements over the cost of Sal & Mookie's. Startup costs that Dan thought maybe Jeff went overboard on some things," Buddy Blumenthal says. "They're probably all necessary, but Dan couldn't see it at the time.

They would fight about the money, but every time Jeff asked for more, Dan would relent. They'd go to the bank and ask to borrow more. And every time the bank loaned it to them.

"It ended up being three times the original amount of money, but once you start construction you can't stop," Dan shares.

"They put a lot of money into someone else's real estate. I wish that I had been smart enough at the time, because I thought there's too much money going into a building that's not ours," Linda Kay Russell says. "Sal & Mookie's has carried a lot of debt since day one, more so than Broad Street."

Dan did tell Linda Kay that they were going to be aggressive with the loan payments. He didn't want to have a loan that outlived the lease on the building.

"Fondren's hot. Jeff and Dan are the reasons that Fondren's hot. You improve an area for people, then they can't afford to live or own a business there," Linda Kay says. "The [Sal & Mookie's] property gets more and more valuable."

"Dan knows numbers and he knows how to project them. If you go over your build-out budget, it's going to take you a hell of a long time to come out ahead in a business that has such a narrow profit margin," Buddy adds.

"Jeff was smart about getting tax credits for opening Sal & Mookie's. This was right after Hurricane Katrina so we got a bunch of write-offs for the depreciation," Dan says.

Sal & Mookie's opened on Friday, April 27, 2007. The 6,000 square foot restaurant had seating for more than 200 people inside and outside, on the large wraparound covered porches.

Once again, people lined up to see the latest venture from Jeff Good and Dan Blumenthal, and the place was packed. It also meant the pressure was high, and Jon Pixler was feeling it. Especially when the wrong thing went out to a table and then came back to the kitchen.

"Guys please, get these tables right," Pixler said to the waitress.

"Shut up and cook the food," she snapped back at him.

"I've never talked to anybody like that at a window ever, and I don't expect anybody to talk to a chef like that, especially when I'm busting my ass, sweating in a 130 degree kitchen," Pixler says of the incident.

It almost led him to quit when it seemed like Dan was taking the waitress' side.

He handed the keys to Dan and said: "Then you run this motherfucker. You run it!"

Pixler walked out of the kitchen, took a few deep breaths and then told himself it was time to get back to work. He walked back to the kitchen, and snatched his keys back from Dan.

"Give me my damned keys back," Pixler said.

Dan didn't say a word.

On the side of Sal & Mookie's, facing Taylor Street, they had created an old-time ice cream parlor that served ice cream cones, sundaes, hand made milkshakes and malts. The guys quickly realized having the ice cream parlor so far away from the dining room was problematic.

If you ordered a milkshake or malt, or a sundae, no problem – the wait staff could go to the ice cream parlor and pick that up for you. But the ice cream cones were another issue.

"The wait staff would have to say 'you have to go get that yourself in the ice cream parlor,'" Dan says.

The restaurant also had a full-service bar, right in the middle of the dining room. That meant guests who were waiting for a table would have to dodge a busy dining room full of families, if they wanted a drink while they waited.

So within the first year, Jeff and Dan swapped the ice cream parlor with the bar.

The new Pi(e) lounge had a swanky vibe that attracted young professionals from all over Jackson. Fondren was quickly becoming the place to be for restaurants and the arts. Fondren First Thursday was a free street festival that would bring new people to the neighborhood on the first Thursday of the month. Afterwards, they would pack into Pi(e) lounge ordering food and drinks.

There were two big drawbacks to Sal & Mookie's though. First, it was just a little too far away from the center of Fondren.

"People feel more trepidations about coming here. We're just far enough off the beaten path that we're just a little outside the Fondren area," Dan explains.

"We're a destination restaurant. Not a lot of people are driving down here at seven o'clock at night," Pixler says.

And then there's the parking problem. The restaurant holds a lot more people than their parking lot does.

"At lunch, parking is an issue. To get in here and back out in an hour is very challenging," Pixler adds.

They have since worked out parking agreements with nearby businesses to ease the parking woes. And it seems to be helping.

Every night you go into the restaurant, and walk down the hallway to the dining room, you see little kids with their faces pressed against the windows, watching pizzas getting made. In the dining room, there's a loud din from families having pizza for dinner. You also see different figures, words and kids' artwork sticking to the walls – all made out of Wikki Stix®, a combination of wax and yarn that keeps the kids busy while waiting for dinner.

In 2017 and 2018, a building boom in Fondren made it even harder to get into Sal & Mookie's.

"They're building hotels and things that will bring people in to Sal & Mookie's, so there's that positive. And I've always liked the restaurant. It's fun," Dan says.

What isn't fun is when they have to close down the restaurant for another "Jackson" problem – no water.

* * *

Wednesday, January 3, 2018
From: Jeff Good
   Team, we just lost water at Sal & Mookie's and all over Fondren. We are NOT opening at Sal & Mookie's today until water is restored.

* * *

Cold Weather Briefing
January 8, 2018
1:00 p.m.
   Water pressures and flows continue to slowly return to normal in many areas within the City of Jackson water distribution network of pipelines as the number of new main breaks has subsided while repairs continue. However, other areas continue to experience low pressure in areas immediately near main break sites, which will have little or no pressure or flow available until those breaks are repaired.

> **City of Jackson continues to be under a system-wide boil water advisory. We anticipate that this emergency will continue due to the number of confirmed breaks that have not been repaired. As of one p.m. today, we have experienced a total of 116 confirmed water main breaks since January 1.**
> [From the Office of the Mayor of Jackson]

* * *

On New Year's Day, 2018 a bitter cold weather system moved into the Jackson area and it stuck around. The next day, the city marked a record low of 14 degrees. Staying that cold for that long meant problems for the city's troubled infrastructure that was already trying to catch up from "deferred maintenance" – meaning the city previously took money earmarked for maintenance and moved it to other parts of the budget. It was a hard lesson the city learned eight years earlier.

In January 2010, Jackson had 154 water main breaks during a deep freeze that lasted four days. In 2018, it was 130 total water main breaks. Both times, the old pipes underneath the ground in Jackson couldn't take the cold and burst, shutting off water to parts of the city, and leaving the rest with low pressure.

Broad Street is in Banner Hall, the highest point in the city, and they're often the first to lose water. Sal & Mookie's is just three miles away, and loses water too. BRAVO! is on the other side of the interstate, and seems to have better luck. It only lost water twice in 25 years.

"With all this water crap going on, not only does the business lose, the employees lost because they couldn't work," Pixler says.

During the entire history of Mangia Bene, they've had to close their restaurants at least ten times: two tornadoes, two hurricanes, the two deep freezes and at least four snowfalls. Every time they have to close a restaurant it costs about eight thousand dollars per day, just in fixed costs.

Having to close because of Mother Nature is one thing. No maintenance in the City of Jackson, that's another.

"When the water went out for four days in Jackson, I got a settlement for us because I made the argument that we were being damaged by a third party peril that damaged the city's water pipes and wouldn't allow us to open," Jeff says. "This is something our insurance agent to this day says 'I don't know how you did that.' I overwhelm them with data in a simple letter, and being a salesman on the phone, being able to walk somebody through it."

Other times of the year, Jackson struggles with the occasional water main break, and that means everyone in that area goes under a boil water notice. Broad Street is hit the hardest and has been under so many boil water alerts they've lost count.

A boil water alert means you can't use the ice machine or the soda fountains. You have to go to paper plates and plastic silverware along with canned sodas and ice in bags. That extra cost for the business is "hundreds per day," according to Dan.

In order to stop the practice of deferred maintenance, Jackson voters went to the polls in 2014. They were voting on the one percent sales tax, which would specifically earmark money for roads, bridges, water, sewer and other infrastructure improvements. Jeff served on Mayor Chokwe Lumumba's committee to promote the vote.

The measure was approved by 90 percent of the voters, much more than the 60 percent it needed to pass. The city started collecting that sales tax a few months later. One percent seems pretty small when you consider the estimated price tag to fix the problem was around a billion dollars.

But it was a start, and Jeff Good wanted more people to be part of the solution. He created a video that went viral on social media called "Pennies for Potholes" where he encouraged people to shop in Jackson, whether they lived there or not.

"A year ago, the city came together and voted overwhelmingly for a solution, a one percent sales tax to dig our way out. When you buy your goods and services in Jackson, you're helping to fix the streets that we drive on. We can fix our streets by shopping at the stores and outlets that sit on these very streets. If we want a better Jackson, then we need to make the effort to shop in Jackson. Every penny counts. Together we can build a better Jackson," Jeff says in the video.

* * *

Dan didn't just get the name of the restaurant from the movie *Do The Right Thing*, he and Jeff also adopted the title as a philosophy, a mantra, inside the restaurant: "Do the right thing." It means doing the right thing when it comes to the customers, employees and as the leaders of the business.

If Jeff needs to go buy office supplies for Sal & Mookie's, or any of the restaurants, he doesn't just go and pull money out of the register.

"Even if that's completely on the up and up, it says 'it's okay to take money out of the till,'" Jeff says. "And that's not the message we want people to take away."

Instead, they have a formal petty cash requisition system.

They're also particular about making sure they "do the right thing" when it comes to paying sales taxes. When a business, like a restaurant, purchases raw product they don't pay sales tax on the front end. The sales tax is supposed to come out on the back end, paid for by the customer with their purchase.

"But when I buy a guest something, like a meal or a dessert, we ring that up as promo. That has no cash or value coming in. It's a sale that is closed out to a promotional account. And it creates a sales tax liability. So we're going to pay the nine percent sales tax on that because that's the right thing to do. The wrong thing to do is to go in and void it, pretend like it never happened," Jeff explains.

There have been times when a potential vendor gives him a quote, but says it's "cheaper if you pay cash" – meaning "off the books." They refuse and are teased for "paying retail." Jeff just shakes his head and says it doesn't matter what everyone else is doing. They're going to do the right thing.

Dan and Jeff also empower their employees to do the right thing.

"People get into cabs and act like cab drivers aren't even there. People sometimes think that the folks who are right beside you, picking up a plate or busing a table can't hear you either," Jeff says. "If a busboy hears someone complain about the meal, we want the employee to speak up. If the waiter pulls the plate and the customer isn't happy, the waiter is empowered right then and there to make an offering to fix that."

Waiters and busboys don't have to go "get the manager" which Jeff believes can actually make the customer more uncomfortable.

"Nothing is worse than when the manager comes over and asks 'what's the problem?' after they just told the waiter," Jeff adds.

Everyone is empowered to take something off the bill.

"Dan and I created this culture, there was no manual handed to us. We created every bit of this," Jeff says. "Have I been taken advantage of? Yes. Have I been lied to? Yes. But it's more important for me to do the right thing and sleep at night, versus worrying that someone got something over on me."

They had to deal with disappointment in 2017, when they found out several employees were stealing liquor and drinking on the job. A manager at Sal & Mookie's was leading it.

"The drinking that had been going on, whether it had been happening every day or not, it happened one day that we know of. We have it on camera. The whole party and him getting drunker and drunker and giving free drinks to people. That's what brought it all down. It wasn't something that happened over time," Dan shares.

The investigation was swift and four people were fired as a result.

When Sal & Mookie's isn't making as much money as it should, the right thing for the business means they go to a wage freeze.

"When it comes to the employees the toughest decisions are having to curtail raises and bonuses when times are tough," Dan says. "Jeff won't make that call because he always believes we can pull out of it."

That doesn't sit well with Pixler, who says that's the one thing he butts heads with Dan about.

"I'm looking at the people I work with and 'X' amount of dollars an hour actually only equates to $24,000 a year. They're 30 years old, they got two kids. I see that," Pixler says. "But I see what Dan is saying. It's a constant battle. I just want to be able to sleep at night because I went to bat for my people. They bust their ass here and do the right thing. They deserve a raise."

"There are times in our history when I've had to say 'look, times are tough. You can't have a raise.' Or 'raises for all employees are halted until I say otherwise,'" Dan recalls.

Dan knows it's better to halt raises and bonuses until things turn around, otherwise they'd likely have to lay people off.

Lesley Tolar became Lesley McHardy in 2002. She had been watching Dan and Jeff's management style since the day they opened BRAVO! together. So when she and her new husband decided to open a wine and liquor store, she knew how to do the right thing from day one.

"They're always doing something. Just because they're not in the restaurant every day doesn't mean they're off at the golf course," Lesley said.

She had watched Jeff and Dan struggle with the Broad Street downtown mess. She watched as they worked nonstop the first few years at BRAVO!, taking a minimal salary, so they could pay back the investors faster. A model she adopted for her business.

"Jeff really taught me that you don't run off to your retirement before you've built your empire," Lesley adds.

* * *

Within a year of opening Sal & Mookie's, Jeff got a call from a young woman who had just graduated from Mississippi College. She was now living in Dayton, Ohio and working for a real estate company.

"I used to live in Jackson and I love your restaurants," she told Jeff. "I've been telling the owners here about it and we were wondering – would you be interested in opening a Sal & Mookie's up here?"

"We don't really have the money to do that right now, we just opened the restaurant and our plate is full. Besides, that would be one hell of a daily commute!" Jeff laughed and they ended the call.

A week later, she called again and asked: "Would you be interested in franchising?"

Within a few weeks, her boss brought a group of people to Jackson to check out the restaurant that the young woman had been raving about. Then, they all gathered in Dan and Jeff's conference room – the two principals of a development company, an architect, a chef and an accountant.

"The architect brought a roll of black paper and rolled it all over the inside of our conference room to make a solid black surface, even the door," Jeff remembers. "This became the idea board."

Jeff and Dan hadn't created a business plan when they opened Sal & Mookie's. The advice Dan had given Jeff at the opening of BRAVO! that there never would be time later to do those things was ringing in their ears as they talked about a possible franchise with these individuals. Jeff and Dan had nothing written down. No standardized plan for Sal & Mookie's.

So they spent several hours going over everything with the team: branding elements, lists, drawings, employee structure, menu items and more.

"I hope you guys are ready to make this happen and I hope you're ready to make a lot of money. You deserve to," one of the principals told Jeff as they were shaking hands goodbye.

"This was going to be our first license. We started talking about the concept, about giving somebody the idea and then they would run it," Jeff says. "We started in the middle as opposed to the beginning because they already had a plot plan for their development."

Dan became really involved with trying to design a restaurant within those parameters and put all the Sal & Mookie's elements in it. They worked for months with an architect, until the end of 2008, when the housing bubble burst.

"The economy fell out and they were in Ohio, which was ground zero. The phone calls stopped," Jeff says.

One good thing that came out of it was the business plan for a franchise.

Rebecca and Bruce Lacey were visiting friends in Jackson when they ate at Sal & Mookie's for the first time. They sat on the porch, and never even came inside the restaurant but Rebecca loved it and thought something like that might be great where they lived, on the Mississippi Gulf Coast.

A friend introduced them to Jeff and Dan.

"Next thing we know, they came up for a visit and they brought their money partner," Jeff remembers. "Then they're doing site locations. They're sending us pictures of different plats of land, asking us what we think."

One place they considered was a strip mall next to Best Buy, and asked Dan and Jeff what they thought.

"Sal & Mookie's doesn't feel like it needs to be on an out parcel next to a hotel on the backside of the interstate," Jeff said.

The Laceys then sent Jeff and Dan a picture of property on Highway 90 in Biloxi, right across from the Hard Rock Casino, and next door to the town park. The only thing left of the building that once stood there was the foundation bricks. Hurricane Katrina had washed the rest away, and the lot sat vacant for nearly a decade.

"This property is for sale," the Laceys told Jeff. "We'd like to put Sal & Mookie's here."

"I remember Rebecca saying 'you know we're going to go big or go home.' And they went big. They built a big building," Jeff says.

"They were focused on their building, their one-and-a-half million dollar building and getting it done right, which is good," Dan says. "But they didn't get the Sal & Mookie's training. It was something we all regretted later."

The Biloxi Sal & Mookie's held a job fair. Jeff and Dan brought Pixler and the front house manager from Jackson for round robin interviews with the licensees.

"We found kitchen managers. We found front house managers," Jeff recalls.

When it came time to bring the staff in to get trained for the grand opening, people started showing up and didn't know anything about Sal & Mookie's. So it became a crash course within a week.

"Dan brought one or two people from the Jackson Sal & Mookie's for the first couple of days," Jeff says. "They went from zero to a full menu of products in two and a half days. I had the front house staff, training them. Then all of a sudden, they start rolling out the food. I couldn't believe it. It was like a parade."

Dan is known for being frugal and watching the bottom line, and when it comes to training, he will often just do a few dishes, so he doesn't waste ingredients. That was not the case in Biloxi.

"Every menu item came out, and it was just incredible. I said 'certainly on the burgers he's only going to send out one.' And then here come three of four different burgers!" Jeff says.

Sal & Mookie's Biloxi opened on Monday, April 13, 2015. Bruce, Rebecca, Jeff and Dan pulled all of the employees outside of the restaurant before they opened the doors to the first customer. The money partner blessed the business with a prayer and Jeff Good gave the team a last-minute pep talk:

"The only way this is going to work is if each and every one of you really lives by the principles that we talked about on Monday, Tuesday, Wednesday and Thursday. We've got to be a different kind of business, where we don't do things the way that we despise them. This is going to be a real tough day. Y'all have never done this before. Our team has been asked to let you guys cook and not take over. But if you get in the weeds, we're there and we're going to help you push through," Jeff told the crowd.

At the end of the two-minute speech, he led the crowd in a cheer of "DO THE RIGHT THING."

"The opening of Sal & Mookie's in Biloxi was really a testament to hard work and caring about what you do. Somebody wanted to replicate what we were doing. They wanted to try and redo it. I was proud. I want them to succeed," Jon Pixler says.

The Biloxi license became a good test of what Dan and Jeff would and wouldn't do in the future. Training in Jackson, for example, would be mandatory for future endeavors.

More people have approached them to talk about licensing Sal & Mookie's, and that may be how the restaurant continues. Especially if the rent goes too high on the Jackson location.

"Finding another location would mean taking on more debt and then waiting for years to make money on it," Dan explains. "When our current loan is paid off in five years and the lease is up, if we don't get a new lease, one option could be to sundown the original Sal & Mookie's in Jackson and let the franchise live on."

BRAVO! Vermicelli
With Roman-Style Shrimp and Asparagus

16 colossal shrimp, tails on
½ cup extra virgin olive oil
6 tablespoons butter
1 tablespoon garlic, minced
1 tablespoon shallots, minced
1½ teaspoons chili pepper flakes
Salt and ground black pepper to taste
⅜ cup white wine
1 cup asparagus spears, sliced on the bias every ½ inch
2 teaspoons fresh mint, julienned
1 tablespoon fresh basil, julienned
1 pound vermicelli (angel hair pasta), cooked al dente
Freshly grated Parmesan cheese and chopped parsley to finish
Bring the oil and butter up to temperature over high heat.

Season the shrimp liberally with the salt and pepper and add to the pan, moving them around as they cook. Add the chili flakes, garlic and shallots, continually tossing the pan.

When the shrimp are about three fourths cooked, deglaze with the white wine and reduce. Refresh the pasta in lightly boiling water. Add the refreshed pasta to the shrimp and toss well. Taste again and add more salt and pepper if necessary.

Serve garnished with Parmesan cheese and chopped parsley.

Note from Chef Dan Blumenthal: This dish is a simple crowd-pleaser that has proved a staple over the years at BRAVO! It is an adaption of the way I learned to make Roman-style shrimp, with the addition of fresh asparagus. It should be oily and rich - that's the point, with the wine there to add a hint of acidity to the garlicky-spicy sauce.

Dan Blumenthal running with the bulls 2002   (photo courtesy Dan Blumenthal)

CHAPTER 6

YIN AND YANG

> **Everything contains Yin and Yang. They are two opposite, yet complementary energies. Although they are totally different – opposite – in their individual qualities and nature, they are interdependent. Yin and Yang cannot exist without the other.**
> **[From "Yin and Yang Theory" by Traditional Chinese Medicine World Foundation]**

It's the last Monday in February, and the entire Mangia Bene office building is bustling. The conference room table has been turned into an assembly line of sorts. Linda Kay Russell, Brenda Tillman from Human Resources and the intern are all stuffing large envelopes, preparing them to mail. Jeff Good bounds up the stairs to his office to get address labels for the envelopes. He brings down one sheet, only to realize he forgot the second sheet of names and addresses, so he runs back upstairs to retrieve it.

These are the Schedule K-1 statements that they mail to their investors every year, and they must be postmarked by February 28. When the envelopes are stuffed and labeled, Jeff will hand deliver them to the post office by nine p.m. tonight to make sure they get to the investors on time.

Jeff ticks off his to-do list: "Yesterday I wrote two letters to investors and had all the financials done. This morning I put together a little collage for the packets."

Jeff doesn't just write the letter and stuff the envelopes. He also keeps track of every investor and any special needs they might have.

"We've got six pages for every investor. It shows their accounts, their capital account, their profit, their loss, their depreciation, their pass-throughs for any tax credits we might have. We've had people who have passed on and their shares were split [between the heirs]. There are some people who have them in trusts or have them in 401(k)s and the original gets sent there, but the investors want a copy. So I go through every page and when I see certain names, I'll make a copy of it."

Jeff takes these extra steps every year, because he feels gratitude for the original investors in BRAVO! and Broad Street.

"Just a little bit of customer service because these people believed in us and gave us our start," he says. "If the worst thing in the world is I need to stop for a minute and scan something or email it because it makes their life easier because they're retired and living somewhere else, then so be it."

Jeff loves a good project, he always has. When he has a pressing deadline, he'll work all night if he has to and get it done – just like he's cramming for a college final. But those projects have to be within his wheelhouse.

"I pretty much stay within the realm of things I can do. I don't do things I can't do, like decorate somebody's party or cook food for a million. But if I stay within the realm of what I can do, I'm capable of getting a lot done," he says proudly.

Jeff has a big personality and tends to be the center of attention wherever he goes. And these days he goes everywhere in the community.

He and Dan are two of the founding partners in Soul City Hospitality, a social business enterprise focused on developing Mississippi's local food economy. Up In Farms was the first result of that partnership, and the food hub is the first of its kind in the state.

Up In Farms "brokers growing contracts for dozens of small- to medium-sized family farms in an effort to get fresh local produce on grocery store shelves, in school cafeterias and on the menus of restaurants throughout the state."

Soul City is also creating the Refill Café, which teaches young people life skills while giving them critical employment experience through the Café's restaurant. Jeff and Dan are both partners in the endeavor but Jeff is the founding principal, meaning he is the one actively involved with making them successful.

Add to that Jeff's packed schedule of emceeing and public speaking engagements, being President of the Else School of Management Advisory Board at Millsaps College, his involvement with the Jackson Chamber of Commerce, a board member of the Greater Jackson Chamber Partnership and being lead organizer for the Fondren Zippity Doo Dah Parade Weekend that raises money for Blair E. Batson Children's Hospital; he's a busy guy.

The walls of his office are covered with awards: 1998 Restaurateur of the Year, 2013 Small Business Administration's Small Businessperson of the Year for the State of Mississippi and the 2014 Governor's Initiative for Volunteer Excellence… just to name a few.

Jeff always seems "on" – moving a mile a minute, working the room, and using his "marketing" voice.

When you meet with him, he mostly gives you his focus, but his phone is constantly buzzing with emails, texts and calls from people all over town. You begin to wonder when he sleeps, and suddenly understand the copious amounts of coffee he drinks every day.

"He does leave a wake sometimes," Dan says of Jeff. "But he is extremely outgoing and very honest."

Janice Blumenthal describes Jeff as "a real dreamer and very positive."

"Tremendous," Lesley McHardy says. "I think that Jeff is tremendous. He's a person who is so passionate about everything he does."

"Passionate" comes up a lot when you ask people to describe Jeff in one word, and so does "Pollyanna".

"He always sees the good in everything and everybody and sometimes it can be a bad thing. But that's the way he sees the world, the way he sees business and that's the way he continues to have the energy to get up every day and go to work and plow through the enormous amount of work he created for himself. He always believes that everything's going to work out for the best, no matter what," Debbie Good maintains.

"Jeff is a 'glass half full' kind of guy. Dan is 'glass half empty' but I'm also like that," Linda Kay admits.

"I would love to be that [positive] person, but I'm not. I'm the guy who's going to say 'look the glass is half empty, fill up the rest.' Jeff is probably going to say 'we've got half a glass of water, we should be really happy! We should celebrate! Let's have a party! Let's put it on Facebook!'" Dan's imitation of Jeff's enthusiasm is near-perfect.

"Jeff is just amazing," Jon Pixler smiles. "His passion, his motivation, his effort. It's ongoing. I try to be the best of both of those guys. The best of Jeff when dealing with people and the best of Dan when I'm setting guidelines and standards of how things need to be done."

Jeff describes himself as "manic" and wonders why so many people have put up with him over the years, especially his wife Debbie, and his best friend Dan.

"Dan doesn't complain. I think about the shit I've dragged him through, just like my wife! I drag these people through all sorts of stuff. I just punish people for being with me. Why would they put up with me?" Jeff asks.

One answer is because his heart is always in the right place. As a result, his friends, family and supporters give him a lot of leeway.

"Most of the time it's positive," Dan says of Jeff's tendency to go overboard with things. "It gets good results. When he's gone too far, I have to step in and say 'look you're smoking hope-ium here.'"

"I think in this business you have to be able to fight it out and work through it and come out better on the other side," Debbie adds. "I don't think it's always easy and there are times when we go through periods where we don't really speak to each other, but it takes that for Jeff to realize, because he's very much a Pollyanna, that everything isn't always rosy."

Jeff does see the darker side of things. In early 2018, the building they chose for the Refill Café was broken into multiple times. Equipment they bought on a shoestring budget was at risk of being stolen or damaged. They chose the location for its proximity to the population they're trying to serve, but when it's attacked, Jeff takes it very personally.

Jackson can be a hard city to love. Thousands of people have moved out of the city in a "white flight" to the suburbs of neighboring Rankin and Madison Counties. State legislators have been reluctant to help the capital city, voting against measures that would improve infrastructure and roads. It's also in a state that is often *last* on the "best" lists and tops on the "worst" lists: Mississippi ranks 51st (the worst) when it comes to people living below the poverty line, children living in poverty, working women living in poverty. It's number one in childhood obesity and number two for adult obesity.

Jeff refuses to give in to the negativity. He often takes to social media to share what's right with Jackson, what's working. When he says, "working together works," it's not just a catchy tagline; it's a personal belief.

"I'm an eternal optimist," Jeff says. "Do the right thing for yourself and for others and hopefully karma takes care of everything else."

Jeff and Debbie have lived in the Jackson city limits for their entire married life. Several years ago they went into the rental business. They purchase run down properties around Fondren and fix them up to rent out.

Debbie says working with him is challenging, because he can be a bit of a "micromanager," but her biggest wish for him is time.

"I wish I could've found a way to keep Jeff from working quite as much and to have been a bit more engaged with the family," she says.

Starting a restaurant business is not for the faint of heart, and often time with your family is the first thing to be sacrificed.

"This is a really difficult business, the hours and the commitment. A lot of people don't understand that there are sometimes years that you don't take a vacation and you work 14- or 16-hour days on average,"

Debbie says. "When Jeff comes home, he's still working. He says he's home, but he's constantly on the computer or on his phone."

Jeff acknowledges that he wasn't always present when he was with his family and plans to make that up to Debbie: "We're spending more time together and I think I need to take it to the next level by surprising her with a trip or something else. We'll get there. We're traveling together, but it's still kid-based."

For years, Jeff had wanted a Currier and Ives-type of Christmas, complete with all the decorations and a party. In 2017, he got his wish. He decked out the house with enough lights to make Clark Griswold jealous and they had a big party for their friends.

Jeff's middle name is Ernest and when you talk to him about his family, his company or his city, you realize it's the perfect description for him. He comes at everything with good intentions, and you want him to succeed.

"I really wish for this dream of his to be able to help Jackson come together and really, really work," Linda Kay says. "This desire to make the city a better city by helping those that live in it, to bring themselves up and improve themselves. I would love to see his dream come true."

* * *

Dan Blumenthal is besieged by a group of young men on the sidewalk outside of Sal & Mookie's. It's not because of his job, but because of his car.

Dan is the proud owner of a brand new 2018 McLaren 720S. The white sports car has a sleek, carbon fiber body and black accents. It has a turbo-charged V-8 engine and with its sexy aerodynamic curves and airfoil, it can hit a top speed of 212 miles per hour, not that Dan has pushed it that fast…yet.

"I'm still breaking in the engine," he says with a smile.

The young men want to hear all about his car, where did he get it? Dallas.

How many others like it in Mississippi? None.

What's it like to drive? Awesome.

Dan patiently answers all of their questions then steps out of the way while they take selfies with his car for social media.

If you didn't know any better, you might assume that 55-year-old Dan Blumenthal was going through a midlife crisis. But you would assume wrong. He's been a car guy his whole life.

He bought his first sports car in 1991, a Honda CRX-SI. When Dan started making money at BRAVO! he traded in the Honda and bought a Ford Probe GT. A year after that, he traded up again – this time for his first Porsche.

"I have a good eye for quality. That's just something I was born or gifted with. I have a love for expensive things," he says.

Dan went through a 15-year period of Porsches. During that time he got his amateur road racing license from the Bob Bondurant Racing School in Phoenix because: "I wanted to take the fast track to see if I could race or wanted to race."

In 2000, he became a certified high-performance driving instructor for Porsche Clubs of America. He took a few days in Nashville to pass the test, which then meant he could teach other people high-performance driving. The perk for that? Being able to drive on various road course tracks for free.

His last Porsche was a beautiful convertible that was painted Mexico Blue. It looked like it had been dipped in the crystal waters of the Pacific Ocean. Mexico Blue is a vintage Porsche color, and wasn't available to the general public in 2013, but Porsche made it available to Dan.

In 2016, he decided it was time to kick it up a notch and bought his first McLaren, the "affordable" 570S. Two years later, he would trade that in for his first real supercar, the McLaren 720S. It joins his "regular" car, a rare BMW 1M coupe.

"This is his way of acknowledging success," his mother, Janice Blumenthal says. "A car, that's his baby, his child. And working is his whole life."

Dan Blumenthal works all the time. On a regular day you see him wearing his "uniform" of a short-sleeved chef's coat and pinstripe chef pants. They're designed for working chefs, and the lightweight material keeps you cool in a hot kitchen.

As the Executive Chef of Mangia Bene, he doesn't have to go into his kitchens, but he does, all the time. He schedules himself to expedite on Tuesdays for lunch at BRAVO!. He does his weekly inspections of BRAVO!, Broad Street and Sal & Mookie's. Then there are the unannounced drop-ins at any of the restaurants at any time, even on the weekends.

"I love it when Dan shows up," Jon Pixler says. "I love working with Dan because he's 100 percent engaged in what he's doing. When Dan walks in, people stand at attention."

Dan's eye for precision in cars is also evident in the kitchen.

"Dan is a perfectionist. That's another characteristic of a chef. And that stamina of his is unbelievable. He's very focused, very intense, very goal-oriented. He's a great leader," Janice says.

The drop-ins aren't because Dan lacks faith in his people; this is more a "trust but verify" trip. He also says "micromanaging every little thing" is his *least* favorite part of being a chef.

His favorite part? The adrenaline.

Being a chef and driving sports cars have that in common.

"Working in the kitchen is a very fast-paced, tense atmosphere. Most of the time a meal period is an hour or two. People come in all at the same time and most of them leave at the same time. Everything is sped up. You need a certain amount of adrenaline to do that. You need to like a little bit of chaos, because it's going to be chaotic."

Dan describes the adrenaline of fast cars and cooking as "satisfying the same part of the brain" and calls them "relaxing" but also requiring a lot of focus and skill.

His love of fast-moving vehicles was also satiated through a series of motorcycles. Twice, he and his chef friends from Jackson took motorcycle trips through Spain to their destination of Pamplona for the San Fermin Festival and the running of the bulls.

> **I'm the first to admit that I'm an adrenaline junkie/thrill seeker. Just ask anyone who has had the (mis)fortune of being strapped in the passenger seat of my Porsche with me at the wheel grinning like The Grinch Who Stole Christmas. However, I would like to think that as I watch my macho teen years fade into the distant past, I have learned to take calculated risks. Up to this point, this "city" boy has never seen a real bull mano y mano, much less put myself in a position to be trampled or gored by six of these ornery, 1,300-pound creatures. So, on this beautiful Spanish summer morning, I thought of what General George Custer had said before going into battle with Geronimo at his last stand – "It's a good day to fight, a good day to die."**
>
> **[From "Fear and Loathing in Pamplona" by Dan Blumenthal, "The Dish" newsletter from Mangia Bene, 2000]**

It wasn't a bull that ended Dan's motorcycle riding, but a domestic creature, closer to home.

"He was over on Woodland Hills and a dog ran out in front of him.

He had to put the bike down and broke his shoulder," Buddy Blumenthal explains.

Dan stayed with his parents after his accident to recuperate. He sold his motorcycles shortly after that, much to the relief of his mother.

With all of this need for speed, he's surprisingly patient and disciplined, especially when it comes to making business decisions.

"I'm going to analyze something before I do it. Before I get you what you need, I'm going to take a look at it. Make sure I'm making the right decision," Dan says.

Lesley McHardy does a great impression of Dan mulling something over, rubbing her chin and slowly nodding her head.

She says: "Dan is going to analyze it from the bottom to the top and side to side. He understands the numbers, he's not a hasty person."

"Dan is patient. You don't expect it because he's so fast and wants to get everything done," Dan's mom adds.

Every month, Dan and Jeff hold managers' meetings with the leaders from each of the restaurants. They go over the financials from the month prior and look at sales and expenses year to year. Dan sits at the head of the conference table, surrounded by spreadsheets and a binder that holds the weekly sales reports for the last year. If there's a question, he knows exactly what the numbers are and where to find them.

"Dan is one of the smartest guys I know. Sometimes when we're in that meeting and he's talking, he sees many things that we're not necessarily looking at. That's why he and Jeff are so different. Dan is the voice of reason. He's also a penny pincher who's not going to make an unsound business decision these days. He sees things differently," Jon Pixler says.

Some restaurants might not share the financials with their managers, but at BRAVO!, Broad Street and Sal & Mookie's, the managers get a bonus based on the "controllable" expenses and restaurant cleanliness inspections – each month, not at the end of the year. Jeff and Dan don't hold it against the managers if the business insurance rates go up, but they do hold the managers accountable for food waste and overuse of electricity.

"When we do the financials, it's Jeff's least favorite time of the month. He gets the numbers, but he's moved on," Linda Kay Russell says. "Dan knows without sales, you have no money. But even there, if he's hard on anybody – number one it's himself. Second – it's Jeff."

"I remember a few years after they opened BRAVO!, it was a Wednesday night, which can be a slow night. Dan came in and just laid down on the floor and said 'I don't understand it. We weren't busy at all tonight. Where is everybody?' And I must have started crying because I felt so badly for him," Janice Blumenthal remembers.

Nowadays, Dan holds the attitude that if things are out of your control, there's no sense worrying about it. But he is going to work as hard as he can on the things he can control.

"I'm unhappy when I'm not succeeding. Or when I don't know what the next step is," Dan says. "Jeff's always telling me to stop and smell the roses, to be happy. But a lot of times that says to me: be happy with what you have, and don't move forward. I'm always looking ahead. The realist in me says there's always more to this life, it's not going to stop here. There's always tomorrow and tomorrow brings new challenges."

Dan is definitely a "work first, play later" kind of guy, and that was beneficial when building the business. It also caught the attention of the James Beard Foundation. Their mission is "to celebrate, nurture and honor chefs and other leaders making America's food culture more delicious, diverse and sustainable for everyone."

When the Beard Foundation invites a chef to cook a dinner for their members, it's a great honor. Dan has been a part of six dinners during his career. He was the featured chef at one dinner at the James Beard Foundation House in New York. He was also featured chef at a James Beard Dinner at a restaurant in the Mississippi Delta. The other four he was part of the kitchen crew for his chef friends, in New York and Mississippi.

Dan has cooked for celebrities and politicians, including: former Mississippi Governor Ronnie Musgrove, Margrit Mondavi and celebrity chef Bobby Flay. He also created the menu and cooked a fundraising luncheon for President George W. Bush and 1,200 of his guests, which included another governor of Mississippi, then Governor-Elect Haley Barbour.

Best Chefs of America is a "national guide to chefs" where chefs nominate their peers for the list. Only the top one percent makes it on the list. In Mississippi there are 26, including Dan. Four other chefs on the list worked under Dan before they got their own restaurants that directly compete with his.

"That's part of the process. You train people and sometimes they leave. It didn't take me long to learn that lesson and make peace with it," he says.

"My partner is the gravitas to our business," Jeff Good says. "He's the anchor. I'm the window dressing, the sizzle to the steak. Dan's very creative and has a lot of skill. There are very few things he can't do. He's very bright."

"I get all the strokes, all the awards," Jeff continues. "And he never complains. He's never bitter about it. He makes fun of me, which is appropriate, but he's never been passive-aggressive about any of it."

Dan has also received many awards during his career. When you walk into his office, one of the first things you see is his medal from the Chaîne des Rôtisseurs displayed in a shadow box. But he can't see it from where he sits at his desk. Those walls are reserved for the numerous plaques thanking him for his help with this fundraiser or that one, from hospice to the Blair E. Batson Children's Hospital to Dining with Dignity.

Dining with Dignity Pop-Up Restaurant is a private event put on by the Jackson Foodies where they provide a five-star dining experience for 200 homeless and food insecure people in the Jackson area. Guests are seated at tables and served gourmet meals from Dan and his team. He has been part of the event since it started in 2015.

"Dan is one of the most critical members of the Dining with Dignity team. Not only does he rise early to begin prep in the back of the house, he then transitions to [expediting] once the restaurant opens for business," said Carlyn Hicks, Founder of Jackson Foodies.

Carlyn said it wouldn't be a pop-up restaurant without Dan because he verifies orders, checks plating for presentation and works with professional and volunteer servers.

"Dan brings that full element of a well-run establishment to this event, ensuring our customers receive their orders with the same effort and culinary pride as they would at BRAVO!," Carlyn added.

Dan has handwritten thank you notes taped to the wall near his desk. And "best of" awards stretch the length of his office, nearly from floor to ceiling. There are national awards and local awards, many from the *Jackson Free Press*. Every year, the JFP releases its "Best Of" list where their readers pick the winners.

"Getting a bunch of *Jackson Free Press* awards, getting best restaurant, best chef, you feel like your customers are standing behind you. It means something, especially when it goes away for a while and comes back," Dan says.

Dan is very close with his parents, who only live a half mile away from him. He has been talking to them about downshifting into a slower pace for the future.

"He is a very caring and lovable person and when he's not working, when he's on vacation with us, he just forgets about work. He's able to get away and relax," Janice says.

Dan also talks about retiring in the next ten years. He plans to keep working to pay off the investors, not necessarily to reach a personal goal: "What do I have left to achieve? In my own mind, it's not a ton. I started fairly early."

"Dan is tenacious. Anything he commits to, he'll see through," Linda Kay says.

"He will never let you down. Dan will never ever miss a commitment.

Dan will be on time, where he says he's going to be, every single time. There's great comfort in that," Jeff adds.

"Jeff is the Pollyanna and Dan is the curmudgeon," Debbie Good laughs as she also describes herself as a curmudgeon. "Like me, Dan is the other person who brings Jeff down to earth, that speaks the truth and usually sees the negative sides of everything. It frustrates Jeff a lot. He'll come home and say 'you know, I wish you weren't so much like Dan and could see the positive in things!'"

Dan prefers the term "realist" to "curmudgeon" and describes himself as "driven".

"That may not be how I describe myself in ten years, but that's been the past 25 to 30 years. Maybe I'll be driven to something else in the future."

* * *

A fellow chef has come into BRAVO! for dinner and starts ribbing Dan almost the minute he sits down.

"Can I get a pasta from 1994?" he asks.

"You sure as hell can. People would kill me if I took it off the menu and it pays for that car out there," Dan points to the parking lot, letting the jab roll right off his back.

It's the sort of thing that drives Jeff crazy.

"He can be friends with everybody. All these people in the industry that may not even like him or like us, but he still remains friends with them. They hate me," Jeff says.

"I try to be lower key than I used to," Dan shrugs.

"Some of the snarky folks in town might make fun of Dan but they're still going to like him," Jeff adds.

Jeff talks about the persona that he's built up, how people refer to him as a Pollyanna and then go after him. But when they threaten the business, he calls them on the carpet and that makes him a target.

"You have to take the good with the bad sometimes. If you want to be out front, to be the leader, you have to take the first bullets," Dan reminds him.

People generally are not on the fence about either one of them.

"Jeff is like me. People love him or hate him, there are not a lot of people in between," Dan explains. "You can ask people about me or ask people about him and there's a lot of 'I love that guy' or 'he'll stick with you through thick or thin'. Then there are people who don't know him well or know me well and they don't like us, for whatever reason."

Jeff seems to have a bigger target on his back than Dan, given the sheer number of events and situations he's involved with.

Lesley McHardy comes across people who think Jeff is "full of shit and will just go back to his mansion and count his money."

"Hold on a second – that guy over there, in the first five years of BRAVO! made less money than I made as a bartender," she tells the naysayers. "I think a lot of people feel like Jeff's just barking all this hot air, but those people don't know him at all."

"Jeff divides people. The people who don't like him mostly think he's just full of bullshit. But he's not. He really is that way – positive and honest," Dan says. "Most people aren't. The people who aspire to be community leaders and politicians say one thing and do another. They're hypocritical."

People who know both men the best never wonder where they stand. And the men inspire a fierce loyalty in their friends and employees.

"I think the world of Jeff and Dan, they're one of the reasons I'm still here," Jon Pixler says. "When I got the job at BRAVO! I was coming from a very dark place. For them to appreciate what I did, that was everything."

As for the chef who was teasing Dan about the menu?

"That's an ongoing joke between several of us. I'm the guy who created that menu item and it's still relevant today. People still want it. And you know what? I still have a restaurant and am driving around in a McLaren. That guy is driving around in a Chevy Malibu," Dan grins.

* * *

Jeff walks into Dan's office without saying a word and dumps a stack of menus on his desk.

"What's this?" Dan asks.

"This is how everybody else is doing a blue plate special," Jeff says, the latest salvo in their war on lunch.

They've been fighting over a "blue plate special" for years.

"I have never done a 'meat and three' or a lunch special that's geared to get people in the door cheaply. I'm not really big on discounts because I think it cheapens what you do," Dan is firm about this.

Dan reminds Jeff that they already have a lunch menu that's similar to the dinner menu at BRAVO!, but with smaller portions and prices. That means similar ingredients to prep each day. But if you add a "blue plate special" only to draw people into the restaurant at lunch, the majority of your regular prep work could be wasted.

But Jeff is relentless when he thinks there is something that will help grow their business. He badgers Dan for weeks until he gives in: "Alright, we'll see how it goes."

"It took him 23 years to get what he wanted," Dan says.

"It brings bodies in, but does it have any effect on revenue and profit? It's way too early to tell. I'm not convinced either way. Our numbers are up a bit," he continues.

The biggest blowups between the partners usually come down to money.

"It's anytime Dan feels Jeff is giving away the store. Usually it's a marketing idea," Linda Kay Russell recalls.

One of the biggest messes was when Jeff decided to do a gift card sale that was a buy-one-get-one, but only for a select few days in the fall.

"I don't think we realized that so many people would get up so early and buy that many gift cards. It was $70,000 and was a one-time thing, but it hurt cash flow for the next couple of years," Linda Kay adds.

Jeff's idea was to reach out to current customers and suggest they buy a gift card for a friend for the holidays, and then they would get a gift card for themselves. The hope was to bring in new business. But that's not what happened.

"The people who did it were already customers, so they were eating for 50-cents on the dollar," Linda Kay says.

Dan thinks Jeff tries to "give shit away" and says Jeff would be happy if there were no prices on the menu.

"To this day I'll tell Jeff 'if you're going to give a discount, no more than 15 percent.' Fifteen percent is where I'm comfortable. Twenty-five percent is not cool, that's too much. Five sounds cheap. There are too many discounts. We don't even know what they all are!" Dan exclaims.

Jeff feels Dan is too rigid and is always pushing him to loosen up on things, even on something as simple as quinoa.

"I'm trying to get Dan to eat a quinoa bowl, to show him how people might want something like this at Broad Street," Jeff starts.

"I had my muffin," Dan interrupts.

"I brought him there to eat a quinoa bowl, and he won't even taste it!" Jeff's voice gets a little higher the more frustrated he gets.

"We had already eaten too much, that's why I didn't try it," Dan explains.

"I try to bring him my prejudices that things need to be new and fresh. I'll get passive-aggressive and say 'look at what all the other chefs are doing.' And his quick answer is 'and I'm still around. I'm not a flash in the pan,'" Jeff says.

"He's trying to do the right thing, even if maybe he's doing it a different way," Dan says about Jeff. "I guess it's just about the respect you hold for your partner that pulls you through the thick and thin."

"I think they've been really good partners for each other because Dan is super-conservative. Jeff challenges Dan, but Dan keeps Jeff reeled in. That's a good dynamic," Lesley McHardy says.

Dan also brings Jeff back down to earth when his ideas get a little "out there."

"Dan doesn't carry any grievances, thank God, because he would have killed me a long time ago. He has a lot to be grievous about with me. Dan is very transactional. He'll say his part and be done. Dan doesn't carry anything with him. He doesn't carry the memory or the stress. He doesn't bring it back up," Jeff says.

"I feel like I can trust him when it gets down to it. I mean that's what has to be the enduring theme that you can trust someone that you're partners and working with," Dan says.

Respect is a word that comes up a lot when you ask about their relationship. It's something their families and friends notice. And it's something they acknowledge about themselves.

"We respect each other," Jeff says. "I just like him. I think he's a funny, funny guy. And it's like a brotherly love that he gives me non-stop shit. God, he gives me shit all the time. Oftentimes it's funny and deserved."

Dan is only four months older than Jeff, and their relationship changes depending on the day. There are days when they are as inseparable as family.

"They formed a bond in high school and they're more like brothers than partners. They fight like brothers," Buddy Blumenthal says.

There are the days when they are teasing each other mercilessly, and pulling practical jokes on each other, like they're living in a fraternity house. Some days Dan acts like the stern father, having to tell Jeff no, he can't have more allowance to go to the malt shop. Then there are times when Jeff steps into the "parent" role, pushing Dan to "go introduce yourself" to other people at an event.

"I don't perk up and say 'hey, that's exactly what I was thinking! I'm going to go be the center of attention,'" Dan shakes his head.

"Dan was also my mentor. I know it sounds really weird since we're working the business together. But anything I needed help with, I'd be able to get the information from him," Jeff explains.

They also tend to stick to their sides of the stainless steel kitchen counter. Jeff takes care of the front house and marketing. Dan takes care of the kitchen.

"They each have their own areas that they enjoy. Dan will say 'let Jeff do that, let him worry about that. And Jeff knows he can depend on Dan to keep an eye on the bottom line," Janice Blumenthal says.

"We play to our strengths. He does things I don't want to do – like watch the bottom line. And I don't step into his world. Sometimes I do, and shouldn't," Jeff says.

One instance of a crossover regards a pastry chef at Broad Street. Their longtime pastry chef had set a high level of excellence and culture and trained her second-in-command. When the pastry chef announced she was leaving because her husband got a new job, Dan looked to the number two to step up.

She told him she was going on a mission trip: "I was planning to tell you, I'm leaving at the end of the year."

"Well damn, that wasn't expected," Jeff said when he heard the news.

Dan started looking for a head pastry chef and hired someone outside of the company. It didn't take long for them to realize it was a mistake.

"The person who came in was disingenuous and started playing a game. When you're incompetent you start to create mayhem, and make everybody else seem to be the problem," Jeff says.

"She had alienated all of her coworkers. Everyone was bailing, quitting and she didn't have anybody to do the job," Dan adds.

Jeff hit the panic button and went to Dan asking him to do something about it.

"We're going to wait and see. We're going to have to let it play out," Dan told him.

"If you continue to let it play out we're not going to have anybody left, because our leaders are losing faith in us that we're not acting on the problem," Jeff responded.

Jeff "wanted Dan to do what's right for the business" and fire her.

Dan was trying to help the woman save her job, or give her enough leeway where she would get herself fired. Then the woman started posting negative things on social media about her coworkers, which is against company policy.

But they had a problem. If they fired the head pastry chef, there wasn't a backup to step into the role, because that person was leaving on her mission trip.

"Damned if you do, damned if you don't," Dan said.

Jeff continued to pester Dan about it, until Dan said: "If you're going to beat me up about it, then you need to help me solve the problem, or leave me alone."

Dan was trying to do the right thing by his employee, but Jeff decided to go for a Hail Mary and talk to the number two person who was leaving.

"I had a heart to heart conversation with her and found out her mission trip fell through," Jeff says. He then went to Dan and said there might be an opportunity to solve everything.

Dan called the problematic pastry chef into the office and fired her.

"It was best for the business," he says.

Jeff didn't tell him "I told you so" or rub it in his face, because he knows Dan doesn't make very many mistakes.

"This is what partners do, so I'm pissed at him for not getting rid of someone sooner who is causing damage, but I understand what he's doing. So, I try to help him solve the problem. I know he does the same thing for me," Jeff says.

"When do I get to be the good cop?" Dan asks. "Not often. But I kind of feel like if I have to be the curmudgeon then maybe I can justify it. Maybe it really is the right thing at that point. I've had to make some tough decisions. I'm that guy. I am the bad cop, because it fits."

"Dan believes in people and he sees talent in people. If he believes that somebody has talent and intelligence, he gives them a broad berth. So he knows that there are some really smart people who have good intentions," Jeff says.

Dan will get mad when someone isn't focused on his or her job. One New Year's Eve, Dan had created lobster bisque, which takes days to make. They were preparing 20 gallons of it for their 180 guests later that night.

"I'd been there all day prepping and making sure everything was just the way it needed to be, and I needed to slip out for an hour or two," Dan remembers.

Before he left, he told his cook: "Stand here with this big long metal paddle and stir the soup. It's on low, but you need to stir it so you don't scorch the soup."

When he returned to the kitchen, he knew instantly the soup was scorched. The cook had gotten distracted and not stirred the soup. Dan was pissed and cussed the guy out.

"There's nothing I could do. I wasn't going to start over, so it became 'smoked lobster bisque' on the menu," Dan says.

"So I have to go re-print a menu at the last minute," Jeff adds.

Dan says the maddest Jeff has ever been at him was on another New Year's Eve. Jeff came into the kitchen and asked for a dish.

"It's right there," Dan points to the window.

Jeff grabbed the plate and it was scalding hot. He got burned then turned to Dan, swearing a blue streak at his partner.

"I think it had been sitting there a while under the heat lamps," Dan recalls.

"On no, you took it right out of the oven!" Jeff insists. "He just wasn't thinking. He wasn't being considerate and it was a stressful night."

It just added to Jeff's aggravation, because it was food for the band.

"We know we have to feed them, but getting food out of Dan every year for the band is like pulling teeth! So when it finally comes out and I'm trying to do everything else, there's this simple thing of feeding the band and you're going to do this to me!" Jeff is still pretty ticked about it to this day.

Dan just shrugs it off because they seem to have their biggest fights on New Year's Eve. They both typically work and it's incredibly stressful, given the effort that goes into preparing for a high-ticket event.

"A partnership, like a marriage, is a sensitive thing," Jeff says. "We do have a partnership agreement that we signed before we did anything else that defines the 'death' of the business. If Dan wanted to quit, or fire me or if one of us became disabled or died, we have an actual legal methodology and some insurance behind it to make sure the business will go on."

There is a process, but they both now have 50-50 ownership of the business, so it's not as easy as it sounds to fire the other one. Not that they want to do that.

"Their partnership is such an exquisite balance that I've never been able to figure out how it has worked so well for so long," Buddy Blumenthal said.

Jeff's father Stuart Good said: "I think it works well because they respect each other to begin with. They have different points of view but they can sit down and work things out."

"I wouldn't be anything without Dan Blumenthal. I might be able to be a good service manager, but I can't cook – at all," Jeff says. "I had to have a partner who knew that side of the business. I couldn't hire that out and vice versa. People don't realize how hard it is to get into business and how important it is to have someone to lean on for skills and support. You can do much more with two than one."

"Jeff will say he couldn't do it without me, and he couldn't in the culinary aspect of it. But he's got everything else wired up, if he chose to do it and if he could focus himself," Dan says. "I could have done the front of the house, no problem. I'm not as gregarious as he is but I could still get the job done, and do it efficiently."

"They definitely need each other," Buddy Blumenthal sums up. "The whole thing comes apart without one of them. I cannot envision any of it working with just one of them doing it."

THE BRAVO! WAY

The respect they have for each other also extends to their employees. And they have had some pretty unique and controversial ways of dealing with personnel issues over the years.

BRAVO! Glazed Chicken Agrodolce

4 boneless, skinless chicken breasts, lightly pounded
½ cup all-purpose flour
Pinch of salt and pepper
½ cup vegetable oil
¼ cup yellow onion, diced
⅓ cup dry white wine
2 teaspoons garlic, minced
1 teaspoon fresh rosemary, chopped
Pinch red pepper flakes
⅓ cup balsamic vinegar

⅔ cup chicken stock
2 tablespoons golden raisins, soaked in hot water for 2 minutes, then drained
¼ cup honey
1 tablespoon unsalted butter, cut into small pieces
2 tablespoons pine nuts, toasted (5 minutes in a 325-degree oven)

Place a medium skillet on the stovetop over medium-high heat.
In a shallow bowl, thoroughly combine the flour, salt and pepper.

Add the oil to the skillet. While the oil is heating, dip the chicken breasts on both sides into the flour and shake off any excess. Place the breasts in the pan and sauté. When the chicken is brown on the first side, turn it over.

Add the onions and sauté for a minute or so. Pour off any excess oil from the pan and add the wine. Be careful, as it may flame since the pan is hot! When almost all of the wine has cooked off, add the vinegar, chicken stock, garlic, rosemary and red pepper flakes.

Cook for another 2 minutes or so. Add the raisins and honey.

At this point, you want to balance the cooking so that the chicken is cooked through and the sauce is reduced nicely. Taste the sauce and add more honey if necessary. If the chicken is cooked through, you may also remove it from the pan to further reduce the sauce if necessary.

Once the sauce is reduced to a workable amount and tastes right, drop in the pieces of butter while swirling the pan to incorporate the butter into the sauce.

To serve, place the chicken on a dish and pour the sauce over it. Top with the toasted pine nuts.

Serves 4

Note from Chef Dan Blumenthal: *This BRAVO! entree has been on the menu since day one — a true BRAVO! classic. It requires a deft hand to get the balance of the hot, sweet and sour ingredients correct, but when you get it just right, it's oh so rewarding!*

Inside the BRAVO! Oven   Photo © Tom and Kasi Beck, all rights reserved

CHAPTER 7

SPEAK TRUTH TO POWER

"Never be afraid to raise your voice for honesty and truth and compassion against injustice and lying and greed. If people all over the world would do this, it would change the earth."
—William Faulkner

The phone rang at Jeff Good's house. It was 6:50 on a Monday morning, and phone calls that early are never good. The front house manager of Broad Street was on the other line, crying.

"I need to talk to you, can I come over?" the Manager asked.

"Sure," Jeff replied.

Twenty minutes later, he appeared at the back door. He displayed eyes that were red from crying, and clutched a washcloth to the face. His clothes were disheveled, and he looked like he hadn't slept in days.

"Are you okay? What's the problem?" Jeff asked.

"Jeff, everyone has problems and I have a bad gambling problem," the Manager began.

For the last several months, the Manager had been taking the bank deposits out of Broad Street and going to the casinos, hoping to win big. Most of the time, no one would have noticed what happened. The employee would take the money on a Thursday night, lose it all, but cover the loss with a paycheck the following day.

In December, he took a tip deposit of $1,910.51 and lost all of it at the casino. Unable to cover that amount, an attempt was made to hide the transaction from accounting.

The Manager admitted to a pattern of taking money from one night's deposit, taking it gambling and returning the next day. If there was a loss, the deposit was withheld from the bank for days until the funds could be replaced. But there were three tip deposits that were held up from January and February that couldn't be replaced.

Linda Kay Russell, the controller of Mangia Bene, has an eye for numbers and knows when something is off. She will turn everything upside down to search for a missing $50, so you can imagine what she would do to find thousands.

"If Linda Kay wasn't here we would have some serious problems. The key is to feed her information in a timely way, and she's going to find it," Jeff says.

When Linda Kay audited the books for December and January that year at Broad Street, she found a discrepancy and called for the operations manager to investigate. The operations manager then reached out to the Manager for an explanation.

The Manager told Jeff that on the previous Friday that all three tip deposits were paid at once to cover up the crime. The Manager met with the operations manager later that day and pleaded ignorance as to where the money was.

The meeting spooked the Manager and led to a misguided gambling binge to win back the entire amount of the missing money. The Manager hoped that would end the investigation.

It didn't go as planned. That Friday night, the Manager took the Thursday and Friday deposits, and lost them gambling. On Sunday night, all of the deposits and $200 from petty cash were lost gambling.

"I tried to win it all back, but I couldn't," the Manager told Jeff. "I don't want to go to jail."

"How much money are we talking about?" Jeff asked.

"$12,000."

The Manager was sobbing and said he thought about killing himself.

"Calm down, everything will be all right. I want you to lie down on the couch, while I make a few phone calls," Jeff said.

Jeff called the operations manager and asked her to come over. Then, he called his insurance agent who would check into what the procedure was for something like this.

"You take out insurance policies and you have coverage for things like this, but you don't want to make a claim, especially with a young business, because your premiums go up," Jeff says.

Jeff called Dan who was blown away by the story.

"It was a lot of money back then," Dan says today. "I had said this business is going to eat us up because of all the moving parts. It's a cash business and you have to have very tight controls on this cash, otherwise it will go missing."

When the insurance agent called back, he told Jeff three things: they were covered for a loss of up to $25,000, the policy didn't require prosecution and it was up to Jeff and Dan whether or not to involve the police.

Jeff then called a former judge who was now a lawyer in private practice. He said the Manager's crime was a felony and each count of embezzlement carried a potential 15-year prison term, 45 years total. The judge told Jeff he had some options: call police and press charges, negotiate an agreement between the employee and the insurance company, and force the employee to seek professional counseling. Jeff called the insurance company back to ask what they preferred.

If you put someone in prison, you don't get your money back, the insurance agent said. Getting the Manager to pay back the money and sign a repayment contract would be up to Jeff and Dan.

"This was a no-win situation. This was a good guy who had one problem. He didn't have a drinking problem. He didn't have a drug problem. He had a gambling problem," Jeff said.

When Jeff quit drinking, he went through treatment and knew a lot of people in recovery circles. He called an addiction counselor, who he had grown close to, and asked about a treatment center for gambling addiction.

"For us not to prosecute, you'll have to pay back every bit of what you stole. You're also going to have to enter an in-patient treatment center to get help for your addiction," Jeff told the Manager. "If you fail to do either of these things, we'll prosecute."

The Manager agreed, and later that week entered the treatment facility.

An insurance company lawyer who drew up the contract between the Manager and Mangia Bene applauded them for trying to do something nice, but said: "this won't work, it never works."

Six years later, the attorney called Jeff.

"I'm holding in my hand the last check. Everything has been paid back," he told Jeff. "The insurance company wants to thank you for that."

"He didn't have anybody at the time to help him," Jeff says of the Manager. "I was empathetic to that. I wanted to help out."

"The manager wasn't hated, and was fairly well liked. I didn't want retribution. I just wanted our money back," Dan adds.

Dan trusted Jeff when he came up with the plan to get the money back.

"When something like that happens on my side of the business, it's my responsibility. I think one of the reasons Dan gives me so much latitude in our lives is when the shit hits the fan, I'm going to take responsibility for it. I'm going to fix it," Jeff said.

"What I love is Jeff's and Dan's desire to help their employees improve themselves," Linda Kay said.

When they opened BRAVO!, Jeff and Dan were only a few years older than their employees. They had worked in restaurants for years and knew the kind of atmosphere they wanted, and more importantly – what they didn't want.

"They knew what they wanted to do. They knew what kind of establishment they wanted," Buddy Blumenthal says.

At first, finding qualified people was difficult. The casinos in Vicksburg hired away a lot of available employees and then there was the education factor. Mississippi ranks last when it comes to educational performance.

"Some restaurateurs might see hiring from that population base as too challenging, and look to bring in people from out of town. But as a member of this community, I wanted to hire the young men and women who lived here," Jeff says.

He believes that has a positive impact on where you live, but you have to understand the world they're coming from.

"It's foreign in Jackson to have an adult listen to a young person. By the same token, it can be foreign to these young men and women to actually tell the truth. They live very complex lives and they're used to having to do a lot of social posing," Jeff explains.

He says "broken" people can also be drawn to working in restaurants.

"They have to create an alternate being for themselves to navigate the very complex world they're living in," Jeff adds.

Some of the people who applied to work at BRAVO! had only eaten at fast-food restaurants with drive-through windows. They couldn't afford to eat at a restaurant with silverware and table service. Jeff and Dan knew they would have to do a lot of training.

"In other cities, you may find employees have an education, some food history or some culinary knowledge. But in my kitchens, you have to train up to that level. You have to see what kind of skills people already have, then enhance those skills," Dan says.

They're also training people on interpersonal skills.

"I've had to learn that when you ask someone a question, they may tell you a fib as a reply," Jeff explains. "What I have found is, people oftentimes are punished for telling the truth, so we try to create an environment where they're not punished."

They wanted people to feel comfortable telling the truth, no matter how big or small it is and even if the truth itself is uncomfortable.

"When you're honest about all things, you can be honest about why you're late to work. You can be honest and know somebody's not going to take money that doesn't belong to them," Jeff adds.

Linda Kay has seen Jeff and Dan teach their employees not just how to wait tables and cook, but also how to treat other people, something they do by example.

"Their heart for their people, I love them for that," she says. "Most people look at Dan and think he looks gruff and mean, but he's got the biggest heart and would do anything for his people."

That includes bailing them out of jail, or loaning them money.

"I can't tell you how many people every year I bail out of jail. One kid decided to fire his pistol in the air and they arrested him. I'm not here to justify it one way or the other, but I'm saying they arrested him," Dan says.

Most of his employees don't have family members they could call when they're in that sort of jam, so they use their one phone call to ask Dan for help.

"In the old days in the restaurant culture this would happen," Buddy Blumenthal shares. "The boss has somebody he'd rather have cooking, than sitting in jail. Even if it costs him money to get him out."

"Without them I can't run a business," Dan adds.

When you ask Dan why he doesn't just hire new people who don't get arrested, he shakes his head. His employees look to him as a father figure, and they're part of his work family.

"He has a good relationship with his workers. It's funny how many times he comes over and says 'I had to lend somebody money,'" Janice Blumenthal says.

"There's something I do that's controversial, which is advance people money. But in order to continue doing business we have to do it," Dan says. "People get paid every two weeks and there's always somebody who's behind."

He doesn't do this for just anyone, nor does he bail everybody out of jail. Dan only does it if someone is a "good solid worker". Then, he makes them pay back the money.

Working in a "closed environment" of a restaurant also leads to shenanigans. Some of it is harmless mischief, like hiding a slice of pepperoni behind a wall clock to see how long it takes the boss to notice. Jeff and Dan recognize that it's a stressful business, and people need to release that stress.

But one area they have a zero tolerance policy for is sexual harassment.

"When we first opened Sal & Mookie's, we had a front house manager we had to let go. He was being completely inappropriate, especially with high school kids," Jeff said.

The complaints came in all on the same day. When Jeff confronted the manager, he denied everything, but was fired. Jeff may be the more outgoing of the partners, but he's quick to fire someone if they're threatening the business.

Another situation was a little more nebulous. Two people who worked in the kitchen together at BRAVO! had been flirty and it had been consensual, until it wasn't. One day the woman was walking through the kitchen and the guy slapped her on the backside, in front of everyone. She complained, and they fired the man.

"We lose someone in a key position, but we sent the right message. And the accuser gets all sorts of grief from the staff because she's not popular, and he was. But we stood by our guns," Jeff said.

He has spent a lot of his free time going through situations like this throughout the history of the company and compares himself to Harvey Keitel's character of "The Cleaner" in *Pulp Fiction*.

"I'm an ad hoc manager. I get involved with it when it happens. I go in and Dan knows I've got his back and that makes the partnership work, because he hates this stuff," Jeff says.

Dan says that's true because "people can be very flighty, and don't always help your cause."

"Jeff runs interference, so I don't have to deal with it. He loves it," Dan adds.

Jeff is also a big proponent of making sure work "works" for their employees.

"The biggest trading chip we have is giving people a schedule that works for their lives. They'll stay with us forever if they can manage their outside lives," Jeff says.

They allow the system to "bend" for people, like the cashiers at Broad Street, some who are single moms.

"Our business hours can be a challenge for their lives. We're a seven o'clock in the morning, open and ready to go business. That means at six o'clock we arrive to set everything up. If you're a single mom, there's a certain set of complexities with that. Yet we bend to be responsive and supportive of the private life of someone, while still having to be on our game – because we've got to open," Jeff explains.

Having a boss that is willing to understand what you're going through in your private life has created employees that would walk through fire for either one of them.

"Dan and Jeff treat their employees like family. If there's somebody in the restaurant that needs something or just needs to talk, someone to talk to, they're really good about being there," Linda Kay Russell says.

Lesley McHardy left to start her wine and liquor store, but still works as the Sommelier at BRAVO!, because Jeff asked her to.

"Jeff is somebody that I'm fortunate to work for. He doesn't even really consider me an employee anymore because we have been together for so long. He taught me everything I know about management. He taught me how to be a leader," Lesley adds.

There are times when the encouragement and lessons they teach can be hard for the teacher.

"Teaching my staff that it's okay to be respectively dissentive. You can speak truth to power. We really want to know what people think, and you're not going to get punished for telling the truth," Jeff says.

It was put to the test recently when Jon Pixler approached Jeff about a training issue at Sal & Mookie's.

"I felt things weren't the same in the dining room as they were in the kitchen," Pixler explains.

He told Jeff he was frustrated that the new servers didn't seem to care about what happened inside the restaurant. It was particularly personal to him, because of all the work he had put into the place to get it open.

"I jackhammered this floor! I put muriatic acid on these bricks. I built that walk-in right there. I put all that grass outside there, I did that," Pixler said to Jeff.

They both talked about the need for more training – for everyone. And not just at Sal & Mookie's. Lesley says it's needed across the board.

"Jeff and I started talking about getting the training back that we went through when we opened BRAVO!. People need to know what Jeff expects, and there are only a handful of us that really knew," Lesley says.

"The crazy thing about this is we're asking people to take the easier way. We're asking people to do the right thing to take care of guests. When there's a problem, buy a meal," Jeff describes the Mangia Bene training.

Jeff says it's totally different from other restaurants where the message is to "protect the house at all costs. Save every penny you can. Never give anything away. Cut, cut, cut."

"What we're saying is the opposite. We watch our numbers, and we're going to talk about labor and food costs, but we don't lead with that.

Today, right now what needs to be done is delighting the guests and have a clean place," Jeff says.

They had to double down on the training in 2001, when another fine dining restaurant opened in Highland Village. Char is a steakhouse with a traditional feel to it. You get the sense that it's the sort of place Frank Sinatra or Dean Martin might have had a meal or a Scotch.

Dan and Jeff were split between BRAVO! and Broad Street, trying to make everything work. But the sales were down at BRAVO!.

"Our leanest year was right after Char opened. That was a hard hit, because you had two high-end restaurants in the same shopping area," Linda Kay Russell says. "Dan would sit in financials and ask 'what if we sold this?' Thankfully we never did."

Jeff wasn't going down without a fight, and it led to a presentation that people would be talking about for years to come.

* * *

Times Change
Time has passed. Things have changed. The recession is real. Competition is FIERCE. Sales are flat. Many of our regulars have become endangered species.

Ladies and Gentlemen we still got "game"

BRAVO! is our baby. It means everything to us…to this end, we are going to RECLAIM the territory LOST over the past few months. How are we going to do it? Focus

FOCUS means to view our business through the eyes of our guests. Everything our guests touch, every transaction, every part of their time with us must say:

- **Excellence**
- **Consistency**
- **Timeliness**
- **Quality**

The Plan: Reclaim our customer base, branch out and gain new customers, make the BRAVO! experience THE dining experience in Metro Jackson.

Every plate is a face. We're only as good as our last meal served.

THE BRAVO! WAY

[From "Every Plate has a FACE," BRAVO! employee meeting, 2002]

* * *

Jeff Good stands on stage at the Jackson Convention Complex. The house lights are dimmed, and the auditorium is filled with more than a hundred employees from BRAVO!, Broad Street, Sal & Mookie's and Mangia Bene.

The Pharrell Williams song "Happy" pumps through the auditorium speakers as people arrive for the 2018 Employee Meeting. Some people just saw each other at work, others haven't seen their colleagues in a while. It feels more like a class reunion than a work meeting.

People settle down and Jeff takes the stage to talk about where the company is right now and where they're going moving forward. Dan Blumenthal sits in the front row, listening. This is Jeff's thing, standing in the spotlight, marketing to the employees.

In 90 minutes, Jeff covers the good – upgrades to BRAVO!; the bad – slip and fall mats aren't where they need to be and other workplace safety issues; and the ugly – a refresher course on liquor liability laws.

The overall theme for the presentation was "It's all about you" – reminding everyone that they were part of a work family and to respect each other, no matter what role they have in the company.

At the end, there was "Do You Want Goat Cheese with That? A Service Story in Three Acts." Jeff brought someone from each restaurant up on stage to role-play and demonstrate service expectations to the team. A side of the stage was set up with tables, chairs and even a faux-counter from Broad Street. It was like having a miniature cross-section of each restaurant right in front of you.

Some employees volunteered to be "customers" and then Jeff gave each of his service experts a scenario to play out. There were some very funny moments when two of the cooks playing customers gave the Sal & Mookie's server some grief with their "order". But she remained calm and smiled through the entire thing.

During the skits, you could also hear employees in the crowd whispering to each other. They weren't having side conversations; they were calling out the next moves. It was impressive.

It was also another moment of Jeff and Dan "catching people doing it right".

The employee meeting was memorable, just like the one in 2002 where the concept of "every plate is a face" was formally announced.

"Jeff is known for his PowerPoint presentations at staff meetings. We picked on him for the PowerPoint, but in the end we were listening. Jeff had this thing and printed off a million copies of it. It was everywhere and says: every plate is a face and we're only as good as our last meal served," Lesley McHardy shares.

It was all about consistency in experience, product and service.

"I'm going to go in and that pizza I had last week that I love so much, it's going to taste exactly the same as it did last week or last year," Lesley says. "It's talking about a level of excellence. We're not trying to be a Michelin star."

"We all thought the training was dorky at the time, but it makes so much sense. All of the stuff that Jeff has come up with over the years makes so much sense," she adds.

When BRAVO! first opened, training was delivered in a one-on-one setting. If you were a server, you would train with another server until you were ready to go out on the floor by yourself. Now, that is augmented by online training.

There is a website for each restaurant that teaches hosts/hostesses, server assistants, waiters/waitresses and bartenders how to do their individual jobs. It also walks employees through a "who's who" in the restaurant and talks about the standards of excellence that are expected.

They also give everybody tests on the food and wine.

"Fill in the blank, the antipasto platter has blank, blank and blank,"

Jeff gives an example. (The answer? Assorted grilled meats, roasted vegetables and cheeses.)

"Risotto is made from what and comes from where?" Dan adds another. (Short-grain rice, like Arborio and Northern Italy are the answers to this one.)

Lesley McHardy will hold a wine class, but these are held during a window of time where they allow servers to drop in and try something new. There's no set time to do it, because that's not how Lesley operates. And it's working. BRAVO! has received the *Wine Spectator* Restaurant of the Year award, every year since 1997.

"As we work on Sal & Mookie's for licensing now the idea of standardization is certainly an important thing, but we've never really been standardized guys," Jeff says.

While Jeff never met a PowerPoint he didn't love to create and share with people, Dan is much more reserved with his time.

"He doesn't want to create something unless he's going to use it," Jeff explains.

Jeff is also very big on giving his managers assigned books to read. When he first assigned *The One Minute Manager* to Lesley, she rolled her eyes at him.

"But I still use stuff I learned from that book and from Jeff. I still use that now running my own business. The whole premise is to catch people doing something right," she says. "We've all had a manager or some sort of a supervisor in our life that all they do is point out what you're doing wrong. You have no respect for them because you just think they suck so bad and it doesn't motivate you to do a better job."

Lesley says that's not the case with Jeff and Dan. She points to Jeff's ability to constantly lift people up by appreciating the job they're doing in the restaurant, and says Dan has his own way of showing his appreciation.

"Dan is a very quiet, stoic man, but he loves his guys back in the kitchen. He takes care of them," she said.

"Money is great, but there's nothing more satisfying than somebody saying 'I appreciate you, thank you so much.' That right there is gold," Jon Pixler says.

When Dan was ready to step completely into the role of Executive Chef, which meant he would no longer be cooking on a daily basis at any of the restaurants, he looked to create a Corporate Chef position. Someone who would oversee the chefs for Dan and also step in at the head chef position as needed. They looked in house and promoted Jon Pixler.

You hear countless stories of Jeff and Dan hand-picking their next leader in a restaurant, because they came up through the culture and knew the right way of doing things.

"There were a couple of good chefs and good cooks when they first opened BRAVO! but there was no culture. They really got all these other people started because they trained their people," Buddy Blumenthal recalls.

The more successful they became at running their restaurants, the more people wanted to know their secret sauce for creating loyal fans and employees. People would call Dan with specific questions.

"Where do you get that piece of equipment or how do you find a chef?" they would ask.

Sometimes they'll ask Dan what it takes to become a chef. And it's advice he gives to anyone, whether they work in his kitchen or not.

"Do as much as possible. I don't want you trained under me, necessarily. I want you to have seen a lot of different things and maybe come back when you've done all that," Dan will tell them.

He encourages people interested in cooking to travel, especially while they're young. He'll say: "Go to Europe, work in various places" because it will expand their culinary knowledge.

"Some people can start as a cook and then they have enough imagination and creativity where they can get what they need through me. But I think a lot of people need to get out in the world and experience what's out there," Dan says. "Looking back, I wish I'd done more traveling prior to anchoring myself in Jackson to open BRAVO! in 1994."

When it came to Jeff, most people ask the more vague questions of: "Can I pick your brain?" or "Can we meet for coffee?"

"It's usually a wanna-be entrepreneur who has a job they don't like but want to do something else. Most of the time it was in the restaurant industry, but sometimes it would be another business," Jeff says.

Jeff would patiently meet with people for an hour and a half as they presented this business idea or another, over breakfast at Broad Street.

"When people come to me to talk about a business idea and they barely have one piece of paper that has an idea drawn out. When they can't write or they don't have the ability to communicate, you can see the challenge they're going to have," he says.

One guy asked to meet with Jeff. He had an idea for a restaurant that also had bounce houses.

"Have you ever run a restaurant?" Jeff asked.

"No," the man answered.

"Have you ever worked at a bounce house company?" Jeff asked.

"No, but it's a great idea, because I have kids and they want to have a bounce house," the man replied.

Jeff shook his head at that one.

Other plans were more thought-out, but had some glaring flaws.

"A well-connected guy came to us with an idea for a beer garden, like the one they have on the Katy Trail in Dallas," Jeff says.

During the pitch, the man laid out the idea for the beer garden that would be located right next to Sal & Mookie's. The man said he could get the money, if Jeff and Dan would run it. Jeff started thinking of the logistics – where to put the walk-in cooler, is there enough parking?

He looked over at Dan who was scrolling through his phone.

The more he did it, the more it aggravated Jeff.

"Why is he being so rude?" Jeff thought.

"I'd like to talk to you about the weather," Dan said when the man finished his pitch. "You've got to consider the weather with this beer garden. The weather in Jackson is 25 percent wetter than Dallas. The weather is 25 percent more humid than Dallas. And the temperature differential in winter is much greater in Jackson."

Dan wasn't ignoring the guy during the pitch; he was taking the Big Picture view of the idea and had looked up the weather averages on his phone.

"I didn't realize it would get that wet here," the guy said.

"It's a great idea, but it would be an uphill battle to get it to work here. You're leaning your ladder against the wrong tree," Dan told him.

"When Dan sees something that makes sense, he sees it clearly," Jeff says of his partner.

All of this "brain picking" and pitching got them to thinking – what if they offered consulting services to other restaurants? So they opened Dollars and Sense Creative Consulting.

"When we were formally out there, we started getting referrals from bankers. They wanted us to meet with their clients who were failing," Jeff says.

They met with restaurateurs who were about to go under. Some of them had money for a consultant. Many didn't. They would cry and pour their hearts out to Jeff and Dan. The guys would offer them some advice, but it wouldn't be enough to save the already-failing businesses.

One day, a chamber of commerce representative called Jeff for his help in Madison, Mississippi.

"We have a new member who's opening a restaurant in a few weeks, would you meet with them and help them get started?" the representative asked.

Jeff went to meet with the couple, who had chosen a location that had once been a cupcake shop. Since the couple wanted to open a restaurant, they had already remodeled and built out a full-blown kitchen. They were going to offer counter service, but hadn't taken into consideration where people would sit to eat.

Their dining room was so small Jeff had flashbacks to Broad Street Express downtown. He got a bad feeling in his stomach. They had already put so much work into the restaurant, before Jeff was even called, but he helped them get ready for their grand opening.

On the day of the ribbon cutting, city officials made speeches, a pastor blessed the business, and then came time to feed everyone. Jeff went inside the restaurant and asked where the food was.

"The ovens aren't even on. There's no grease in the fryers," the cook told him.

Jeff wasn't even sure there was grease in the entire restaurant. But they did have some parts of the lunch ready for people to eat. Jeff went back outside and grabbed the microphone.

"Opening a restaurant can be exciting and hard all at the same time! Sometimes we get so caught up in the excitement we forget to do things, like turn on the oven!" he made light of the situation to ease the tension in the crowd. "We're going to treat you to lunch and we want to invite you back for dinner tonight!"

Later that night, as it often can be with a brand-new restaurant, the dinner service was a complete mess. It didn't take long for the couple to realize their kitchen was configured all wrong. After they closed, Jeff helped them rearrange their kitchen to be more functional.

"I got an electrician in. I got a plumber in. We had to move a lot of things around," Jeff describes.

The next couple of weeks, Jeff was at that restaurant all the time. But there was a big glaring problem: he wasn't paying attention to his own restaurants, something Dan was getting on him about. His own managers were also speaking their "truth to power" and telling Jeff he needed to get back in the restaurants and pay attention to their business.

The client's business didn't survive. And it wouldn't be long before Jeff realized his own businesses weren't going to make it if he kept going like this.

"I was in the shower one morning, worried about another client's company. I was worried about what I was going to do for him that day," Jeff admits.

It was a wake-up call for him. Dan and Jeff got out of their short-lived consulting business shortly after that.

"People had great ideas that needed to be really fleshed out. What they needed was a business consultant to walk them through the process from idea to business plan to opening the business. That's not what we were interested in doing," Jeff says pointing to business incubators who do that now.

Dan says the biggest mistake most people make is underestimating what it will take to open a business, whether it's a restaurant or not.

"They just don't have a clue as to how hard the work is. What it's going to take to do it. If you go in with the mindset that you're going to work your butt off, then you're probably going to be okay. But if you go in thinking it's going to be fairly easy, then it'll go wrong," he says.

Dan says to be a success you have to put *personal* investment into it, whether that's your own money or time or both. That's how they created BRAVO!, he and Jeff were in the restaurant non-stop for five years.

Jeff will also use the BRAVO! story to showcase the persistence it will take to be a successful business person. He's not ashamed of the hard-won wisdom from their failures. Jeff is very candid when he talks to people, and if there's an idea he thinks will absolutely fail, he will tell that person "don't do this" and hope it sticks.

He doesn't do it to be mean. He does it to try to save someone from the anguish of having a business fail if they haven't gone through all the steps to create a business plan, flesh out the concept and think through all the nuances of the business.

"We did the work and that's how we got it done," Jeff says about BRAVO!. "Nobody had really done what we did ever before, especially for a restaurant in our market. It's just a very different model. It took grit. We just stuck with it and kept on doing it until it was done."

When Jeff re-focused his efforts on their business, the three restaurants and the catering division, his employees and managers were glad to have him back.

THE BRAVO! WAY

People still call Dan and Jeff to ask questions or for advice or to ask them to invest in a business. They patiently listen and do what they can, but remain committed to doing the right thing in their own business, and leading by example.

* * *

April 23, 2018
Re: I'd like to give you a compliment
Comments: On Saturday, after buying a piece of blueberry cheesecake for my grandson's dessert, I left my wallet at the counter. When I realized it about 10 minutes later, I inquired at the counter and was informed that the person taking my order had secured my wallet and it was in the safe. The manager had already called my wife to report the found wallet, using the phone number on my business card.

My wallet was promptly returned to me with all the cards and cash inside. I had been to the ATM that morning and had $120 in cash. I'm a regular customer and have always counted on Broad Street to provide excellent food and service. I'm very appreciative of your staff's honesty, and that is another indication of what an excellent organization that makes Broad Street a great restaurant. Thank you very much!

[Feedback email from Broad Street customer]

Photo © Tom and Kasi Beck, all rights reserved

BRAVO! Citrus Olive Oil Cake (Italian Pound Cake)

3 cups all-purpose flour
1 tablespoon plus 1 teaspoon baking powder
1 teaspoon salt
3 cups sugar
6 large eggs
1 orange, zested
2 lemons, zested
2 teaspoons vanilla extract
1 tablespoon amaretto liqueur
½ cup milk
1½ cups olive oil

Preheat oven to 350 degrees (330 degrees for convection oven).

The ideal pan is a false-bottom angel food cake pan. Spray the pan with a non-stick coating.

Mix the flour, baking powder and salt together in a bowl. Set aside.

In a mixer with whisk attachment, beat the sugar, eggs, and citrus zests until pale and fluffy. Gradually beat in the milk, oil, vanilla and amaretto. Add the flour mixture and beat just until blended. Pour into prepared pan.

Bake for about 50 minutes, or until a skewer inserted into the middle of the cake comes out clean. Do not open the oven during the cooking process!

Makes one cake.

Note from Chef Dan Blumenthal: To be perfectly honest, this was one of the least-ordered desserts at BRAVO! over the years, yet one of my favorites. I think people just didn't understand it. Similar to a good pound cake, it is best-enjoyed slightly warm, with some macerated fresh berries and fresh vanilla-scented whipped cream.

BRAVO! Grand Reopening 2017
Front Row: Dan Blumenthal, Jeff Good. Middle row: Lesley McHardy, Patrick Munn, Lindsay Burton, Phyllis Calvin, Tara Washington, Alphonso Campbell, Tanya Burns, Lauren Williams, Antonio Tino
Back Row: Geoffrey Harper, Christopher Robertson, Josh Stanbaugh, Preston Owens, Daniel Schmidt, John Damron
Photo © Tom and Kasi Beck, all rights reserved

CHAPTER 8

THE BRAVO! WAY

June 8, 2014
We have a worsening problem in the kitchen at BRAVO!, specifically on the hot line just in front of the expansion joint in the building. The building has obviously shifted and caused the tile to crack several feet and is dangerously welling up at that area. It appears to be a [Highland Village]/building issue, so I'd like you or one of your guys to take a look at it so we can plan a course of action to remedy it, before it does more damage.
Thanks,
Dan
[Email from Dan Blumenthal to Highland Village Management]

In 2014, BRAVO! had just celebrated its 20th anniversary. The restaurant had been in the same spot at Highland Village since it opened, and during that time the shopping center flourished. High-end shops opened up.

A big coup was when Whole Foods came to the Jackson metro area, and instead of building a store in the Madison or Rankin County suburbs, they chose Highland Village in Northeast Jackson.

Highland Village now had twice as many stores than it had when BRAVO! held its grand opening. But there was a problem. BRAVO! wasn't just showing its age in the décor, it was falling apart at the seams.

BRAVO! wasn't like any other store or restaurant in Highland Village. The kitchen was built on the south parking lot. The lounge was on the second floor of the main building and the dining room was on the bridge in between. The dining room was connected to the kitchen part of the building by an expansion joint. This would expand or contract depending on the weather and allow the dining room to safely float back and forth. The expansion joint also kept things steady during windy days.

It was built that way for The Sundancer, and after 40 years, the steel holding it all together had become damaged and malformed. The kitchen started moving south, away from the dining room and lounge. That was causing the kitchen floor to twist and buckle, creating a hump in the kitchen that went right through the hot line area.

The cooks in the hot line were tripping over the hump, and they complained. One sent Dan a text: "We have to do something about floor on the hot line. Everyone's back and knees are beginning to bother them. You may be without a crew…"

That twisting also created cracks in the floors. And every night when BRAVO! cooks took apart the kitchen to hose everything down, some water would leak down into the barbershop below.

"We had used up the useful life of the building, it was just plain old," Jeff Good says.

When Jeff and Dan looked around at the restaurant that they poured their blood, sweat and varicose veins into, they hardly recognized her. They had a big decision to make. Renovate or move. Their lease was coming up at the end of 2017, and that would be here before they knew it.

For most of their time at Highland Village, Jeff and Dan would deal directly with the owner of the development, Mr. Fowler. He believed in them and had been an original investor in the restaurant. After he passed away, the family sold Highland Village to WS Development, a company out of Massachusetts that managed properties all over the country.

Jeff and Dan had heard from their fellow tenants that WS Development was going to double the rent, but they hadn't received anything official, so they called a meeting.

The first leasing agent came in like a hurricane. She talked very fast and referred to a thick binder that she brought with her. She opened up the binder and told them they had to do something soon, because their lease was coming up at the end of the year.

"No, our lease is up at the end of 2017," Jeff said.

"No, it's 2014!" she insisted.

Jeff told her to take a closer look at the lease, and sure enough, its end date was 2017. The meeting ended without her offering solutions to their building problem. Jeff and Dan felt like they were put "on notice".

Not long after that, WS Development sent a new leasing agent, one that took the time to get to know them better and learn more about the community.

"Tell us what you want to do," Leasing Agent Number Two asked Dan and Jeff. "Do you want to remodel? We would love for you to remodel!"

"It could take months for us to remodel this place," Dan said.

"What about moving to another location within Highland Village? You could get that place ready while still operating BRAVO! then you wouldn't miss any sales. You'd just move over when it was ready to open," Leasing Agent Number Two said.

"That's an interesting idea," Dan nodded.

The woman suggested the Julep location, a restaurant that had recently closed. It was located on the north side of Highland Village, at the corner of the frontage road for Interstate 55 and Northside Drive. Getting in and out of there was challenging, and parking was practically non-existent. The guys shot down that idea.

"How about the Albriton's Jewelry location and the Polka Dot

Pony?" Leasing Agent Number Two suggested. "You could combine the two spaces. But, if you move, you'll have to pay for it, and basically build a new restaurant."

"The conversation opened up at that point because we had some time to figure things out," Jeff says.

They promised to discuss it and get back with her. She wouldn't have to wait long for an answer.

* * *

> September 29, 2015
> Re: Moving forward
> Our interest here is to move forward as quickly as possible. We have two years left on our lease and we are going into our busy season now. We'd like to have a plan of attack sooner rather than later.
> I have spoken with Jeff and we both agree that moving the restaurant, while a great idea operationally, would be prohibitively expensive – we have no idea where we'd get and pay back the million(s) it would take to do a NEW, first-class restaurant.
> So, with that in mind, our biggest area of pain going forward is the kitchen area. The plumbing, floors, walls and most importantly the expansion joint are all worn out and need to be refurbished. To do this we realize we are looking at some shutdown time, but it will probably still be less costly to shut down for a month and pay some of the kitchen remodeling than to build an entirely new space. Any changes to the dining and bar areas could be handled by us during that "shutdown" period.
> We see the expansion joint as a major engineering issue. So the bottom line is we'd like [Highland Village] to engineer and design/oversee the refurbishment of the BRAVO! kitchen. This would allow BRAVO! to continue safely operating well into the future and would justify us signing a new lease at a higher rental rate going forward.

THE BRAVO! WAY

Thanks for keeping an open mind and working with us.
Dan
[Email from Mangia Bene to WS Development]

* * *

Jeff and Dan met again with Leasing Agent Number Two to focus on fixing their current space. One of the most immediate issues was an air conditioner for the kitchen that had quit working.

"If you pay for fixing that, we'll work out the lease," Dan said.

"Sign the lease first, then we'll fix the air conditioning," the leasing agent replied.

Dan thought they could get more help out of the company, but they would have to hold off on signing a new lease. So Dan and Jeff replaced the air conditioner unit out of their own money.

"We have a couple of options here," Dan told Jeff. "We can do nothing, sign a short-term lease and ride the building into the ground. We then sundown BRAVO! when the lease is over. Or, we could bite the bullet and renovate now."

Jeff and Dan had figured this day was coming, and had given the BRAVO! limited partners a heads-up. The last cash distribution was made in September 2014. They then started setting money aside for a renovation.

Just as they were beginning to work things out, WS Development called a meeting with all of the tenants, to introduce themselves and talk about the plan going forward.

Many tenants were concerned about a rent increase, but for those in the courtyard, they had an additional issue.

"One of their biggest concerns was what would happen with the fountain," Jeff says.

The fountain was a Northeast Jackson icon. It was in the middle of the Highland Village courtyard and shaped like a Celtic cross. There were crisscrossed bricks topped by four lions in the center. During prom and senior picture season, you'd be hard-pressed to get close to the fountain, because every teenager in Northeast Jackson was there – capturing their rite of passage in front of the water.

The man from WS Development talked for an hour to the tenants and swore, "Nothing is going to happen to the fountain."

Three days later, temporary fencing went up around the fountain and it was demolished. Several long-time tenants were already fed up with rent increases, and this was the last straw. They left.

Not long after, WS Development reassigned Leasing Agent Number Two, and sent Leasing Agent Number Three to talk to BRAVO!. At first, she was rather dismissive. Jeff and Dan thought they'd have to start all over, building a relationship with someone new. But after talking with them, Leasing Agent Number Three became friendlier and more positive – working to find a solution to keep BRAVO! in Highland Village.

She brought in the developer's construction manager, Lee Shain. He was out of Massachusetts, and had worked with several of the company's developments on their renovations.

"Do you want to make cosmetic changes, or really get things fixed?" he asked. "It's going to take a minimum of 90 days, no matter what you choose."

Dan knew they could no longer put another Band-Aid on the problems, because they had some safety issues that needed to be addressed in the kitchen. But they couldn't close for three months.

"90 days is too long. This is like a delicate operation. If you put the patient on the table and it takes too long, he could die," Dan said.

"We have to get that time down," Jeff added.

"Well, if we do that, to make it successful, we can't go to bid. You're going to need to pick a contractor and have them walk us through it, together," Lee told them.

Jeff and Dan chose Mid-State Construction. That was the firm that did the original build-out of Broad Street, and they felt comfortable with Mid-State's work.

Mid-State and WS Development worked out the entire project, and got it down to a 30-day construction cycle. One specialty vendor would work on the foundation while Mid-State gutted and remodeled the kitchen, fixing the structural steel issues.

WS Development decided if they were going to put that much work into the building, they wanted Jeff and Dan to remodel the front of the house. Lee came to Jeff and asked: "who's going to handle the front house remodel?"

"We're not doing a 'remodel' we're doing a 'refresh'," Jeff told him. "We don't have the funds to do an entire remodel, but we'll do our best."

If they got everything done within that 30-day period, WS Development would give BRAVO! $134,475 for improvements to the space.

* * *

Wednesday, July 19, 2017
From: Billy Ware
To: Jeff Good, Dan Blumenthal
Re: BRAVO! Kitchen Renovation
Jeff and Dan,

Attached is the schedule we have developed for the kitchen renovation. This schedule is based on a 6-day x 10-hour workweek. That is not to say that those are the only times people will be working, because afterhours is the float needed to keep up the work. Sequencing is critical. The activities have to happen in proper order. There are several activities that will only allow one trade to be working at a time.

Note: I understand that you guys are eager to re-open after the renovation, however I feel it is highly risky to schedule a major event too close to the projected completion date. I would recommend a little breathing room after the work is complete.

Thanks,
Billy
[Email from Mid-State Construction to Jeff Good and Dan Blumenthal]

THE BRAVO! WAY

* * *

Erik Kegler knew all about construction sequencing. He and his partner, Brennan Hovell, had recently opened Erik Kegler Interiors in the building next to Banner Hall. They also happened to be long-time customers of BRAVO!.

Jeff went to them and shared the ambitious plan of shutting down the restaurant for 30 days, fixing the structural issues in the back while they "refreshed" the front. Erik and Brennan came back with an elaborate design, and a quote of $200,000 to do everything. Dan said they could realistically get a $100,000 bank loan, and Jeff told the designers to cut the quote in half.

Dan also said it was going to cost them $75,000 in wages to keep everyone on the payroll, while they were shut down.

"We can't afford to close and not pay our people because we need them back immediately when we reopen," Dan told Jeff.

Not only would they lose those employees who had been part of their work family for years, BRAVO! would have to hire all new people. Then it would take time to train them, and teach them the culture. Jeff came up with the idea to utilize the employees for the labor needed during the "refresh." He had no idea just how much he would need their help.

Erik suggested they get rid of the old wood top tables, chairs and everything else, through an auction. Jeff got a case of déjà vu – taking him back to when they were clearing out The Sundancer space in 1993.

"Erik and Brennan came up with every kind of way that we could make money while we were closed like auctioning off all of the old furniture and fixtures in BRAVO! and auctioning off dinner parties in people's homes," Jeff says.

They also suggested holding a big party – a closing party. Sell tickets, give away the good wine in the cellar and let people say "farewell" to the old BRAVO!

THE BRAVO! WAY

* * *

From: BRAVO! Italian Restaurant & Bar
Date: July 25, 2017
Subject: Time For Us To Say Goodbye...
...Goodbye for now, that is.
We're renovating!!

The past called us the other day with some important news: 1994 wants their chairs back. So we're going to RENOVATE!

From August 28th through September 25th we will be CLOSED to give BRAVO! a clean, modern look that honors everything you love about her.

And of course we're throwing a wine party to celebrate. Because we're BRAVO!

"The Closer" Party:
- August 12th from 6pm until the good times end. We ain't shutting this party down until we want to.
- We'll be pouring rare, vintage wines from our cellar all evening

You have to be at The Closer in order to bid on your favorite seat for The Unveiling in September. There will be NO OTHER WAY to attend the reopening.

We will also be hosting an auction for a piece of BRAVO! history. All furniture and accessories must GO! Love that table? Want that lamp? Place your bid and you might just get to take it home with you when we shut down August 28th.

[Email sent to the BRAVO! mailing list]

* * *

The word was out. BRAVO! was shutting down for a month, and the entire city was buzzing about it. The story was splashed across the news and social media. Naysayers didn't believe the place would only be shut down a month, predicting construction delays and the eventual death of the business.

The BRAVO! fans weren't listening to those people, and lined up to buy their tickets to The Closer. It was so popular, the party sold out and there was a long waiting list.

When it came time for the party, this would not be one of those "fashionably late" types of affairs. The BRAVO! regulars knew if they wanted to taste the most expensive wine left in the cellar, they had to be there when the doors opened. By 6:15 p.m. that Saturday evening, people were lined up along the walkway to check in.

After customers checked in, they could either go inside, or walk to the left on the outside balcony to look through BRAVO! news clippings and photo albums through the years. Then, a professional photographer was set up to take your photo, just like you were at a wedding, or on a cruise.

Part of Erik and Brennan's business is Eventful, where they design intricate partyscapes for high-end events. They took over the BRAVO! space for The Closer, removing all of the tables and chairs. They redesigned the space, bringing in high-top event tables that were draped with a silky green fabric and topped with a metal lantern with a candle inside.

"That dining room that I could walk through blindfolded was transformed into something different, something special," Jeff says.

Partygoers packed the place dressed in a variety of styles. Some people wore shorts and sandals, others were dressed up, complete with their bling. The noise was overwhelming. People had loud conversations just so someone standing right next to them could hear what they were saying. Old friends and longtime fans of BRAVO! would point out places in the restaurant where some of their rowdier memories had been made, then gales of laughter would sweep through the crowd.

"I've never seen BRAVO! like this," one woman said.

"This is an interesting layout of the restaurant," said another.

"They're really going to do something different here," their friend observed.

Dan had started the evening in the kitchen. He was overseeing the food, to make sure everything was just right.

"I knew how important this party was," he said. "I wanted to make sure we had enough food because this was a major event."

Wave after wave of servers came out of the kitchen carrying heavy appetizers and sweet treats. They held their trays high, trying to make their way through the crowded room.

Wine lovers stood four deep at the wine station, where Lesley McHardy poured "the good stuff" and answered questions. Everywhere you turned, you ran into someone else you knew.

Even though it was 90 degrees with 80 percent humidity outside, and the front doors were wide open, Jeff Good was wearing a tuxedo with a red bow tie. He was in his element, floating between one group and the next.

"There were so many people there. It was amazing. It reminded me of the exorcism party," Jeff says. "One of the best parts of the night was having Debbie and our daughter Carly there."

Debbie Good doesn't often come out to events at BRAVO! but made an exception this night.

"We had a blast that night, drinking wine and visiting with people. My closest friends were there. Carly was there. It was just fun seeing everybody," she said.

Jeff went to pull Dan out of the kitchen, so he could mingle with everyone. They both were mobbed, and could barely move through the crowd, so many people wanted to talk to each of them. Even Dan enjoyed the party.

"I knew it was important to bring attention to what we were doing, the renovation. It was important to have a party to celebrate that," Dan shares.

Midway through the festivities, Jeff announced the auctioning off of seats to The Unveiling party that would take place sometime at the end of September.

THE BRAVO! WAY

"Some of you have been with us since the beginning. Some of you are newer friends to BRAVO!. Dan and I want to thank you for coming out tonight, and supporting us all these years. We are truly grateful you are here," Jeff said.

He capped off his speech with a special thank you to Debbie and planting a big kiss on her right in front of the crowd. Everyone cheered and whistled.

"People were hugging and kissing me. There was so much adrenaline. So much positivity. It's one of the best nights of my life," Jeff says.

The plan was to hold an auction for The Unveiling seats, but the crowd was just too big and too full of wine for an orderly auction. So they posted the seating chart for the event and let people fill in where they wanted to sit.

Then the band played. By the end of the evening, everyone was a sweaty mess from dancing, laughing and celebrating their favorite restaurant. Around midnight, BRAVO! staffers poured their last glass of wine, handed out their last appetizer and sent the last guest home in an Uber.

That's when the hard work began.

* * *

August 11, 2017
Commitment to our Employees
How we will pay staff members during the construction shutdown

The purpose of this memo/contract is to address pay for each of you during our shutdown phase, August 28 – September 26. Our intention is to pay each and every one of you during this period, at the normal two-week interval. Your pay will be calculated and paid out at your regular base wage, multiplied by the average hours you work per payroll. Tipped employees who make less than minimum wage for their base wage will be paid at a higher wage to make up for tips.

Jeff and Dan are proud of the fact that we are committed to each and every one of you – our work family. This offer to pay you in full during the downtime is testimony that we care. We want to fix BRAVO!, make it new, and open it back up at the end of September together, with you. Jeff likes to say "Working Together Works" and we must agree there has never been a time where his saying is more apropos.

Now for the details: In order to receive your pay, we are requiring that each of you work at least your average hours per payroll doing whatever odd jobs we might have for you, including, but not limited to: moving equipment and furniture out of and then back into the restaurant, cleaning of all kinds and minor painting, decorating and carpentry work as needed.

If you sign this contract, you are agreeing to come back to work with us when we reopen and continue to work with us for at least two payroll periods following reopening. Failure to return to work will result in the forfeiting of any unearned time on the clock.

[Contract between BRAVO! and the employees during the 2017 remodel]

* * *

Employees stood around Jeff Good on the morning of Monday, August 28. This was the first day of an intense month of renovations within BRAVO! and before that work could begin, they had to demolish or remove almost everything from inside the restaurant.

The temperature was lower than The Closer party, but humidity was hovering around the 100 percent mark, and it started to rain.

From hostess to busboy, dishwasher, cook, bartender, wait staff and managers... Jeff led everyone as they removed tables, chairs, lights, bar stools, kitchen equipment and more from the restaurant. They brought it all out into the Highland Village parking lot. Because of the rain, they had to set up pop-up tents to keep certain things dry.

The Closer party brought in nearly nine thousand dollars from the auction alone, and those items were set aside for the "winners" to pick up.

While the employees were clearing out the restaurant, plumbers and electricians got to work disconnecting everything. Lesley McHardy supervised the boxing up of all the remaining liquor and wine as they cleared out the bar.

When the blinds were removed from the west windows, Jeff had the team paint the outside of the windows black. He didn't want any "spoilers" getting out ahead of the big renovation reveal in a month.

On the floor, underneath the tables was commercial carpeting that had been glued down to the concrete, years ago. Employees took crowbars and heavy-duty scrapers that looked like flat shovels to scrape up the carpeting, roll it up and toss it in the construction dumpster outside.

In the bar area, there had been an incredibly awkward and uncomfortable booth built where The Sundancer's fireplace once stood. The back of the booth created a half wall that stopped you when walking in the front door at BRAVO!. The team took sledgehammers to this, removing it altogether.

By the end of the first day, you could barely recognize the restaurant. The team had been hard at work since eight o'clock that morning, and they called it a day around nine that night. Jeff had been documenting the day with his phone, and posted the photos to social media before he went through emails and listened to the voicemails left by people all day long.

After sleeping a few hours, he went back to start the next day of renovations.

"Every morning, it felt like the beginning of *Mission Impossible*. Erik would give me the 'mission should I choose to accept it' – the instructions for that day that had to be followed to the letter to stay on schedule," Jeff explains.

The instructions were very specific.

"I want you to paint these items and use five coats of varnish," Erik would tell Jeff.

Then there were certain touches Erik would do himself, like the barstools. When the stools were painted black, he hand-painted gold flake accents to each one, making each one unique.

That night, Jeff recorded a series of videos for his manager Patrick. He was leaving a set of instructions for Patrick, because Jeff and Dan were taking the next day off. They had tickets for a concert out of town, and would be back the following day.

"See those barstools over there?" Jeff said on his video, as he swung the camera around to the stools. "I want you to get fresh plastic and cover them up in the morning and make sure they don't get damaged or chipped."

When Patrick got the videos, he texted back and told Jeff not to worry, he had everything under control. Jeff and Dan left for the concert.

The next day, Jeff came into BRAVO! and pulled off the plastic. The barstools had been painted solid black - again.

"Patrick! What happened?" Jeff cried.

"The barstools had these weird gold scuff marks all over them, so we repainted them black," he answered.

Jeff shook his head, and Erik told them to sand the stools back down and start over.

The employees sanded the bar down to the raw wood and stained it according to their instructions for the day. But when Erik came in the next morning, he said "wrong color" and made them start over.

Two and a half weeks into the renovations, Jeff started to get very punchy. That was the day of the brass hinges.

The front doors to BRAVO! had brass hinges that had been there for nearly 25 years. During that time, they've never been really cleaned or repaired, so they had rusted.

"See those hinges? I want you to sand them down until they're shiny," Erik told Jeff.

"Why can't we just paint it oil-rubbed bronze, like everything else?

No one is going to see them!" Jeff complained.

"I will. I will see them. People will notice them," Erik said and handed him sandpaper.

Jeff would struggle getting the rust off the hinges, but in the end he appreciated Erik's attention to detail.

"He pushed me to be better and pushed for quality and consistency. He made us redo things over and over until we got it right," Jeff says.

The team was "refreshing" everything in the space. They removed the seats from the barstools and reupholstered them. They removed the railings from the windows and spray-painted them. They spray-painted trashcans and light fixtures. They went through hundreds of cans of spray paint.

One of the biggest complaints Jeff would hear about BRAVO! was it was too noisy on a busy night. Initially, they were going to remove the white ceiling tiles and paint them black, but a customer of BRAVO! called Jeff and said he had a special order of acoustic tiles he would sell Jeff for much, much cheaper than it would cost him to buy retail.

"What color are they?" Jeff asked.

"White," the man answered. "But you can paint them any color you want, as long as you use a certain type of paint."

They set up a paint station in the parking lot outside of Highland Village. For two days, passers-by got a rare glimpse at the renovations going on inside. Regulars were really excited to learn the acoustic tiles would dampen the sound inside.

One thing that didn't get demolished or removed was the 30-foot mural in the lounge done in 1994 by Lynn Green Root. It was an iconic part of BRAVO! that everyone agreed should stay, especially since Lynn had passed away in 2001, just a few days before her 47th birthday. Jeff carefully covered the mural with plastic to protect it from the renovations.

Before they started the renovation, Jeff said he was going to be very hands-on with the project. Dan agreed to oversee the kitchen renovations and give Jeff as much labor as he needed, while he worked on the menu and kept an eye on their other restaurants.

But Jeff seemed to forget about their bargain, and was getting on Dan's last nerve.

"One of the big rifts that Jeff and I had during that time was: I wasn't game to kill myself in one month. I'm in this for the long run. I wasn't pushing at 100 percent during the remodel, because I had certain things to get done," Dan explains.

He would check in on the kitchen renovations twice a day. Dan was also reworking the BRAVO! menu, from the ground up.

"I've never combed through the whole menu looking for consistency and wording," Dan admits. "It had been pieced together over the years and the descriptions weren't consistent."

His task was to remove some items from the menu, add some others. And he was also preparing to add his version of a "blue plate special" which was more of a "quick lunch" - three lunch combos that they would offer for eleven dollars each.

A lot of that work was done behind the scenes, and when Jeff didn't see Dan in the front house, he would get "crispy" about it.

"It was never my intent to be there on premises, 24-7, sanding baseboards. I did very little of that stuff and I think he resented that to a degree. He was just single mindedly focused and if you weren't on his train, you weren't on the train. He went a little overboard," Dan says about Jeff.

Jeff admits he was also "misbehaving" at home.

"I was just becoming a real asshole because I never slept. I was there eight o'clock in the morning until eleven p.m., every day. I would go home, spend another hour on the computer just to bang out stuff to catch up, and then go to sleep. Get up and do it all over again," Jeff shares.

You could see it on his face. There's a telling selfie on Facebook where he's looking off in the distance. It was captioned: "Forty-yard stare on Day 20."

Jeff wasn't just getting too little sleep, he was also losing weight, because he wasn't eating. His Facebook fans could watch him lose weight before their very eyes as he posted pictures each day. But he was close to the end and knew he would have to push through to get it all done.

By Sunday, September 24, the kitchen was done and prep started on the food for The Unveiling.

On Monday, September 25, Jeff posted a picture of the certificate of occupancy issued that day by the Building Department in Jackson.

"This says it all. Our formal certificate of occupancy! Exactly 30 days from start to finish…a complete gut and remodel of the kitchen, a top to bottom renovation of the dining room and service areas, we did it!" Jeff wrote on his Facebook page.

"I've never heard of anybody doing what they did, using their staff and building a family. Not only getting the work done but also having all of their staff invested in the institution. Keeping them employed during the shutdown," Buddy Blumenthal said. "I really don't know how they managed to pull everything together. We've done renovations, major ones, and they never finished on time. They finished BRAVO! on time."

There was still work to be done in the dining room, and Jeff and his team would be working right up to the moment people came for The Unveiling party.

* * *

September 21, 2017
From: BRAVO! Italian Restaurant & Bar
Subject: You asked for it – The Unveiling menu is here!

BRAVO!'s big reveal is just around the corner.

Want to be the first to get a glimpse? Grab your tickets NOW for The Grand Unveiling.

This will be a truly spectacular five-course dinner, including wines, this coming Tuesday, September 26th for $200 a person. You can choose whether you would like the early seating at 6 PM or the later seating at 8:30PM. See the menu for yourself below, grab some friends and get tickets while you can!

    BRAVO! Grand Unveiling Menu
Tuna & Salmon Tartare
Heirloom tomatoes / salmon caviar / avocado / pea shoots / cilantro oil / root vegetable crisps
2016 Domaine des Berthiers Pouilly Fume Saint-Andelain – Loire Valley, France

    Oyster & Fennel Bisque
Lemon oil / fennel pollen / Parmesan crisp
2016 Wente Eric's Chardonnay Unoaked, Small Lot – Livermore Valley, CA

    Louisiana Crawfish & Mascarpone Ravioli
Brandy cream / house-made bacon / black truffles / heirloom toybox tomatoes / tarragon / shaved Parmesan
2015 Loring Wine Company Pinot Noir – Santa Barbara County, CA

    Wood-Grilled Skirt Steak
Duck fat-braised Brussels sprouts / fingerling sweet potatoes / chanterelles / smoked sea salt maître d'hôtel butter
2014 JC Cellars "Smoke & Mirrors" Red Blend – California

    Molten Belgian Dark Chocolate Cake
Gorgonzola cheese gelato / chili gastrique / vanilla bean whipped cream
Ferrari Carano "El Dorado Noir" Black Muscat – Russian River Valley, CA

[Email sent to BRAVO! mailing list]

* * *

Hours before The Unveiling dinner, last-minute work was being done in the dining room. Jeff, Debbie, Erik and the rest of the team were putting the finishing touches on everything. The blinds that had been ordered for the west windows were too sheer, and it was too late to get new ones. That meant the six o'clock seating guests would be dealing with a full-on sunset shining right in their faces.

Tickets to the event were steep, $200 a person, and as a result – fewer people had purchased tickets than Jeff and Dan hoped. They decided to rearrange the seating so everyone could sit in the dining room close to the kitchen.

Before they shut down for the remodel, Jeff had taken a series of pictures with him in a tuxedo, "pulling back a curtain". It was used to create a big sign outside of BRAVO! and all the marketing materials, building buzz for the grand unveiling.

The night of the reopening, black curtains were set up at the end of the walkway, so guests would have to walk through the curtain into get to the restaurant.

About an hour before the guests were set to arrive, Jeff called everyone out to the parking lot. He had the entire crew line up for a picture, just like they had taken on the day BRAVO! opened. Dan and Jeff stood in the same spots they did in 1994. Then, picture time was over. It was time to get ready for their guests.

The first people through the curtain that evening were blown away by the transformation. When you walked through the front doors, the first thing you noticed was that the lounge was now completely open. High-top tables and chairs had replaced the terrible bench. There were regular-height tables and chairs as well, in the lounge. The bar area had been painted a sophisticated gray color that highlighted the bottles on the walls.

On the floor were vinyl planks in blues and grays that alternated throughout the entire restaurant. To the right, the large booths had been reupholstered with a dark blue vinyl. The ironwork lights had been replaced with "starburst" fixtures that bounced light everywhere. At the tables were upscale chairs with varying upholstery, some were solid color beige on the front with a blue pattern on the back, and others had different blue patterned upholstery.

Each table was topped with a dark blue table runner, wine glasses, bread plates and rolled up cloth napkins in a tan color. Everything seemed to sparkle. Servers circulated with trays of sparkling wine for the party-goers. And every time someone new entered the room, you could see their eyes go wide as they took in all of the changes. Some gasped at the transformation and said: "It feels different, but it's the same!"

Buddy and Janice Blumenthal were at the first seating that night and were also amazed at how things looked.

"I think they hit a home run with the renovation," Buddy said. "They've enhanced the atmosphere. It's more comfortable now, more hospitable."

"The ambiance is so warm. It's totally different but I love it," Janice adds.

Everyone was walking around the restaurant, snapping pictures for social media until they were seated for dinner.

The word was out, and BRAVO! was about to face a huge crush of customers who wanted to see the stunning transformation for themselves.

"When we re-opened I made a pledge that I was going to be there for the better part of the first week because I knew what it would take to rebuild the restaurant," Jeff says.

Jeff was making sure everything was in the right place in the front of the house, while Dan was getting the back of the house in order.

"New shelving and everything, you've got to find new places for everything. Things lying around need a new home and then teach people where to put things," Jeff adds.

The first week back open, BRAVO! was packed every night. By the time Friday night rolled around, there were so many people waiting to get into the restaurant, just to put their name on the list, they were backed up out on the balcony. They had added more tables out on the balcony, but those were full as well.

In the bar, people were standing five deep to get a drink while they faced the long wait for their table. BRAVO! may have a new look, but their rule of no reservations was still intact.

There were so many people, you began to wonder if BRAVO! was getting close to its fire code occupancy limit!

Jeff worked the dining room, just like old days, going from table to table thanking people for coming out and supporting them. Dan was in the kitchen, expediting and making sure the new menu items were prepared and plated correctly. It reminded him of those early adrenaline-fueled days in BRAVO!, and he realized he "didn't miss them that much".

BRAVO! was the "hot new restaurant" again, but Jeff and Dan were making sure they continued to be consistent in what they do.

"Certain industries are constantly reinventing themselves, just to reinvent themselves. Let's use Nike for example. Who says one year from the next that the shoe they made in 2017 is not just as good and cool in 2018? But they'll totally shelve it and do something new," Dan explains.

"Is food that way? Does it just have to be changed because it *has* to be changed? Or is veal piccata something that we can keep on the menu forever and do it well?" he asks. "There's a very fine balance between this. People love 'new and shiny' but they also like something they're comfortable with."

Dan believes you can take classic items and add newer flourishes to them to stay relevant without losing your customer base.

Staying true to the customers is at the core of The BRAVO! Way.

"It's superior service, food and dining experience," Linda Kay Russell says.

"Do the right thing and care about what you do," Jon Pixler adds.

"The BRAVO! Way is very genuine, authentic. It's not snooty. We're not going to create a long list of lineage of all the items that go into your special. We're just a comfortable, consistent experience," Jeff says.

THE BRAVO! WAY

Everyone talks about BRAVO! as being a personality-driven restaurant, pointing to Jeff and Dan. But the restaurant has its own personality, one that people are fiercely loyal to, from the customers to the employees.

"I always refer to the restaurants as 'mine', but that's the way I feel about them. Jeff wants his employees to think about them that way too, and treat the customer like they would if they were in their own home. Customers are the most important things to us at any given time," Linda Kay says.

"My three restaurants are like three children, they all have different personalities," Jeff says.

"I care about BRAVO! like it's mine and I hope in 20 years it's still going just like it is," Lesley McHardy says. "I think BRAVO! has the potential to pretty much just be there forever."

"Broad Street will go on for a while because it has to. Sal & Mookie's could be hamstrung by the lease. But BRAVO! is different. BRAVO! is a personal thing and I want to be the one who decides how it goes on in the future," Dan shares.

Whatever its future, Dan and Jeff will decide it together as they have made all decisions in the last quarter century. They may have different personalities, but they share a passion and drive for the restaurant dynasty they created together. It's a rare thing, finding a partner who is just as persistent as you are, so when you find someone like that, you stick together until the end.

The BRAVO! Way might be best summed up by this paragraph written by Jeff Good for a consultant. They were discussing creating a new mission statement for the restaurant, and this is what Jeff came up with:

> **BRAVO! is more than a restaurant ... it is an attitude. It is the affirmation of excellence. At BRAVO! we strive for unparalleled quality and absolute precision in every step of our service. We source the finest raw ingredients, prepare them by hand using our creative recipes and time-honored processes, and serve attractive, flavorful creations to our guests with confidence and grace. We**

hold in high regard the local honors and national awards to which we have been bestowed, and we uphold a company culture, which celebrates and rewards personal excellence and collaborative effort.

Photo © Tom and Kasi Beck, all rights reserved

BRAVO! Flourless Chocolate Torte

18 ounces semisweet chocolate, good quality
6 large eggs, at room temperature
8 oz. heavy whipping cream
Cocoa or powdered sugar to finish

Preheat oven to 425 degrees.

Prepare a 10-inch false-bottom cake pan with non-stick spray and place a wax paper circle in the bottom. Place on a square of aluminum foil and fold the sides up so the torte won't absorb water in the hot water bath. Place the chocolate and cream in a plastic bowl and melt in the microwave, or melt in a metal bowl over a double boiler on the stove.

Place the eggs in a 5-quart mixing bowl and whip on high speed until the eggs gain enough volume to reach to the top of the bowl (5 to 10 minutes).

Pour the chocolate/cream mixture into a large metal bowl. Fold the egg mixture, in two batches, into the chocolate.

Pour the batter into the prepared pan. Place the pan in a one-inch-deep hot water bath, and place in the preheated oven. Bake for 5 minutes. Lower the oven temperature to 400 degrees, cover the top of the torte with foil and bake an additional 10 minutes.

Pull the torte out of the oven, take the foil off the top and refrigerate. Dust the top with cocoa or powdered sugar. Cut into quarters, then cut each quarter into thirds or fourths.

Serves 12 to 16

Note from Chef Dan Blumenthal: If you like chocolate, this is the perfect dessert. If not, don't even bother. It's gluten-free, not too sweet (no added sugar) and it's definitely a crowd-pleaser.

Author's note: It certainly pleases me. It's my favorite dessert!

Acknowledgements

I knew the day I became a BRAVO! regular because the waitress brought me my favorite glass of wine, before I even ordered it. She then smiled and said: "Miss Dawn, I went ahead and set aside a piece of flourless chocolate torte for you!"

My love of that restaurant and its great service began long before I became friends with Jeff Good and Dan Blumenthal. And when I learned their philosophy behind that superior service, it ruined me for other businesses. Their restaurants became the yardstick by which I measured everything else. Jeff and Dan were my muses for this book. They were incredibly frank about their successes and failures and patiently sat through hours of interviews while I captured their stories. They agreed to give me full access with nothing off limits - and they held up their end of the bargain - especially when Jeff opened his hoarder's closet full of material from the last quarter century.

I want to thank Debbie Good, Janice and Buddy Blumenthal, David Blumenthal, Lesley McHardy, Jon Pixler and Linda Kay Russell for sitting in the hot seat and allowing me to grill them for hours. Their perspectives were invaluable and some of their stories are still making me laugh.

The amazing cover art was done by Suzi Jochimsen Hood. Sheila Hennis got me comfortable in my own backyard for my picture. And thank you to James L. Dickerson and Mardi Allen from Sartoris Literary Group who saw the same great story in BRAVO! that I did and wanted to publish it, so the rest of the world could read it, too.

Finally, special thanks to "my people"—my friends and family who talked me off the proverbial ledge when the book became real. It's a tall task to take on the telling of the BRAVO! tale, and if you're going to do it, you can't screw it up. My parents, my brother and my best friends were tireless sounding boards and test kitchens for what I've written. I hope you enjoy reading it as much as I enjoyed writing it.

Bibliography

"About Us." *The Chaîne des Rôtisseurs*. https://www.chaineus.org/

Carbin, Greg. "1997-1998 Winter Weather Events." *NOAA/National Weather Service Storm Prediction Center*. http://www.spc.noaa.gov/obswx/winter/winter.html

Eason, Brian. "9 in 10 Jackson, Miss. voters approve 1% sales tax." *USA Today*. 15 January 2014. https://www.usatoday.com/story/news/politics/2014/01/15/jackson-ms-sales-tax-vote/4489851/

Eliot, T.S. *Prufrock and Other Observations*. London. The Egoist Ltd. 1917

"Infrastructure 1% Sales Tax Program." *City of Jackson*. http://www.jacksonms.gov/index.aspx?NID=665

Johnson, L.D. and U.S. Army Engineer Waterways Experiment Station Soils and Pavements Laboratory Vicksburg, Mississippi. "Properties of Expansive Clay Soils: Jackson Field Test Section Study." May 1973. http://acwc.sdp.sirsi.net/client/en_US/search/asset/1047348;jsessionid=123F059D923858EABE0EE9C98F482F0A.enterprise-15000

"Regulations for obtaining use of the collective trade mark 'Verace Pizza Napoletana' - (Vera Pizza Napoletana)." 2008. *Associazione Verace Pizza Napoletana*. http://www.pizzanapoletana.org/public/pdf/disciplinare%202008%20UK.pdf

Traditional Chinese Medicine World Foundation. "Yin / Yang Theory". *TCM World*. https://www.tcmworld.org/what-is-tcm/yin-yang-theory/

THE BRAVO! WAY

About the Author

Dawn Dugle is an award-winning storyteller who spent more than two decades as a broadcast and digital journalist. During that time, she saw great stories that weren't getting told, so she quit the news business and made it her life's purpose to tell and share the good things that are going on in our world. Dawn is a Mississippian by choice, twice. She has written for *USA Today*, the *Austin American-Statesman,* the *Clarion-Ledger,* and the *Jackson Free Press.* She is currently employed as creative director at SuperTalk Mississippi, a talk radio network that covers the entire state of Mississippi.

THE BRAVO! WAY

www.ingramcontent.com/pod-product-compliance
Lightning Source LLC
Chambersburg PA
CBHW071609080526
44588CB00010B/1071